Lynda Field is a trained co̲_____ specializes in personal and _____ author of eleven titles, includ_____ *Amazing* and *60 Ways to Cha*_____ seminars and workshops, she runs a telephone and on-line coaching service, and writes articles for a variety of national magazines. She lives in Essex, UK.

Visit Lynda online at www.lyndafield.com

Praise for *Be Yourself*

'Take control of your life and improve your self-esteem with the help of this encouraging book – and learn that life is to be loved and not simply survived'

Here's Health

'Inspiring'

Woman's Way

'For more ideas, read *Be Yourself* by Lynda Field'

Best

'Reading *Be Yourself* by Lynda Field will help'

Deirdre Sanders, *The Sun*

BE YOURSELF

How to Relax and Take Control of Your Life

Lynda Field

Vermilion
LONDON

5 7 9 10 8 6

First published in 2003 by Vermilion,
an imprint of Ebury Press, Random House,
20 Vauxhall Bridge Road, London SW1V 2SA

Random House Australia (Pty) Limited
20 Alfred Street, Milsons Point, Sydney,
New South Wales 2061, Australia

Random House New Zealand Limited
18 Poland Road, Glenfield,
Auckland 10, New Zealand

Random House South Africa (Pty) Limited
Endulini, 5A Jubilee Road,
Parktown 2193, South Africa

The Random House Group Limited Reg. No. 954009

Papers used by Rider are natural, recyclable products made from wood grown in sustainable forests.

Printed and bound by Mackays of Chatham plc, Kent

A CIP catalogue record for this book
is available from the British Library

ISBN 0-09-188753-4

Contents

This book is dedicated to my wonderful mother Barbara Goronwy. Words can't express my gratitude!

Acknowledgements

THANK YOU

To my wonderful family, who keep me on track and show me what is most important in life. I love you all very much.

To my friends, who are always there for me.

To my clients and colleagues, who remind me that there is always another book to be written.

And to Judith Kendra, my brilliant editor, and all the team at Ebury Press.

Introduction

What is this life if, full of care,

We have no time to stand and stare?

W . H . D A V I E S

It can be a busy life, and who would wish it otherwise? But while we all want fulfilling and stimulating experiences, we can sometimes get so carried away by the pace of our lives, that we become too busy to stop and enjoy ourselves. If our days and nights are full of things to be done, how can we ever find the time to know ourselves and to love our lives? And if we can't stop to appreciate the world and each other, what can be the point of all this frantic activity?

Be Yourself is for anyone who feels that they are so busy trying to get their lives 'sorted' they might have forgotten their true purpose. The demands of this material world can keep us rushing about – doing this and that, playing one role and then another – until one day we can find ourselves on a hamster's wheel, going round and round in circles and unable to get off. Excessive activity in pursuit of the desire to 'have it all' and 'do it all' can make our daily reality feel like a relentless routine. Life is here to be lived and loved, so step off that wheel and look around you; you are so much more than you think you are. You can do what you want to do and be what you want to be and still relax and enjoy the trip: you can be successful and happy without struggle, strain and stress.

Of course it's not such a simple matter to 'be yourself', is it?

Who are you behind the many parts you play and the multitude of emotions you feel? *Be Yourself* takes you on a journey to find the real you: the 'you' who exists at three interdependent levels of being: mind, body and spirit.

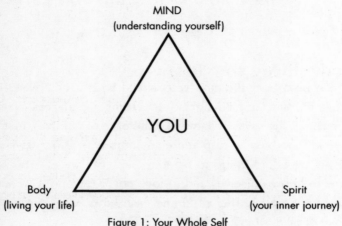

Figure 1: Your Whole Self

Figure 1 is a diagrammatic representation of your whole self. You are more than your mind, more than your body and more than your spirit: the real you exists where you operate in balance and harmony at these three levels of your being. Figure 1 demonstrates the interconnectedness of the three aspects; each supports and connects the others, and none can stand alone. When you are equally in touch with your mind, body and spirit you are at one with yourself and the rest of the universe and your life feels meaningful and purposeful: the whole you is the real you.

For a moment let us consider your Mind, Body and Spirit as three separate categories.

Mind (understanding yourself)

Who do you think you are? Why are you running around in circles? What exactly do you think is the meaning of your life? *Be Yourself* seeks to answer these very personal questions and to show you how to understand yourself and your motives using simple self-reflective techniques. Self-knowledge opens the door to effective change; begin really to know yourself and take control of your life.

Body (living your life)

And what of your physical presence out there in the world? Are you an optimist? Do your relationships work? Are you a go-getter or do you sometimes feel like a victim? Can you make effective decisions and follow them through? Actions speak louder than words and *Be Yourself* focuses on your behaviour and its consequences. Discover some new positive life strategies and learn how to make things happen.

Spirit (your inner journey)

Be Yourself also takes you on a fabulous path of spiritual self-discovery. Heaven is not a place but a state of mind that you can create every day of your life. Joy lies within and cannot be bought; learn how to connect with your Higher Self and feel this joy: it is your birthright. With easy and inspirational techniques you can experience the true depths of your real self. This journey will help you to find inner calm and peace, enjoy it!

But the energies of your mind, body and spirit are insepara-ble, as if linked together with invisible thread. The rich tapestry of your life is created by every strand you have ever woven, by every thought and every action. Everything is connected and

Be Yourself is written in a way that expresses this connection. Each chapter is linked to all the others but can also stand alone, so you don't necessarily have to read this book from beginning to end; you can simply dip in whenever you have a few moments spare – to unwind, be inspired and get motivated.

Never forget that you have a unique place in this world. Find your true self and you will live your best life. Just *Be Yourself*.

1
Who Do You Think You Are?

'It is never too late to be what you might have been.'

GEORGE ERNST

A friend asked me how I could be writing a book about how to be yourself when his whole problem was that he didn't know who he was. And this of course is exactly the point. We are complex multi-dimensional characters dancing about on the stage of life in a variety of costumes and performing numerous roles; how then can we begin to know our real self?

We all have some idea of who we are: what we look like, the type of person we think we are, our likes and dislikes, our abilities and weaknesses ... and then of course there is the person we want to be! Our goals and ambitions for ourselves imply that we don't really have such a fixed idea of self; we know that it is possible to change and to expand our horizons. We only need look around us to see the incredible possibilities offered by the human experience: people are extraordinary, original, powerful, creative and inventive, and we all want a life less ordinary. We all want to reach for the highest within us, to be the most we can be, to give it our best shot, to feel satisfied and fulfilled by the life we have created, to be balanced and aware and in touch with the true purpose and meaning of our existence. This book demonstrates how we can each rise to our full potential and live a happy and successful life.

Step out of the box

Our personalities are complex; we have many voices and conflicting thoughts and emotions. We believe what we have learned to believe about ourselves and our world, and we often find that these beliefs stop us moving forward. If you are plagued with a pessimistic disposition then it might be good to know that you can change it. If you are stressed and overburdened it really is possible to step beyond this feeling and regain control of your life. Perhaps in the attempt to have it all you are finding yourself having to do it all, but it doesn't have to be like this for you. It really is possible to relax and take control of your life. Hard to imagine? Well start now! Open yourself to infinite possibilities, realize that you have a purpose on this planet, know that you attract whatever you focus upon the most, be ready to step out of the box and become your true self!

Our personal vision of who we are can keep us stuck in the same old habits and grooves. But comfort zones are only comfortable until we outgrow them, and then we feel confined, trapped and uncomfortable.

This process (of moving on) is a natural one; we change, progress and evolve throughout our lives, and the trick is to be able to move along with this natural flow. Of course change can often feel risky and threatening, and when it does we are inclined to hold ourselves back by creating self-imposed limitations.

The ways in which we restrict and limit ourselves are not always easy to detect because they are locked into our belief systems. Look at the following list to discover any of the ways in which you might be restricting your own potential.

Ways in which you may be limiting yourself

Low expectations: You get what you expect. What do you expect for yourself? What do you think you deserve? Circumstances and people walk through the doors of your expectations so watch what you expect.

Glass ceilings: This is another form of low expectation. Why do you believe that you can only go so far, be so good, achieve so much? You are the only person standing in your way. Only you know where you have constructed your glass ceilings, but if you keep pointing them out to other people (by expressing your lack of self-belief) then soon everyone will know where they are.

Belief in scarcity: Prosperity is abundant, nature is prolific and love is everywhere. We are all connected in the most profound way; we are all here to cooperate with each other. A belief in scarce resources grows from fear and creates a need to compete. Impoverished and limited thoughts create a poor and mean life. Embrace abundance, love and trust.

Unhealthy boundaries: Your boundaries delineate your sense of self. If you don't know who you are, how will you ever know where you end and another person begins? Good, productive relationships depend on knowing where you stand and where you draw your lines in the sand. You cannot have a good relationship until you know yourself, so maybe you need to get your boundaries sorted out.

Reluctance to change: Whenever we feel threatened we naturally try to protect ourselves and so we often resist any change that exposes us to something new. But don't take this too far. Check: is this change good for me? Why am I fearful? Are my fears realistic or unrealistic? Sometimes opportunity knocks and we have to take the plunge or miss the boat.

EXERCISE:

Beyond self-limitations

In her wonderful book *You Can Heal Your Life*, Louise Hay includes a visualization that she calls the Ocean of Abundance. I borrow from this image for this exercise that will help you to go beyond your self-limitations.

Imagine that you are standing on the beach at the edge of the ocean. You look out to sea and know that the ocean represents the abundance that is available to you in your life. What container have you brought with you: a spoon, a bucket with a hole in it, a paper cup, a baby bath, a bath, a sieve? Think of your container as your consciousness (the more you can imagine the more you can have). Of course you could connect a pipeline to this ocean of abundance and then you would have an unlimited supply.

There may be many on the beach with all manner of containers, but the amazing thing is that there is always enough to go round: the ocean cannot be emptied and there is enough for everyone. Imagine this fabulous ocean of abundance as often as you can and remember that you can always bring a larger container (your consciousness is infinite). Embrace this feeling of unlimited expansion and let it into your life. You can be all you want to be. You can have all you need. Expand your self-expectations.

Reflections

- You can have it all without having to do it all.
- You attract whatever you focus on the most.
- Comfort zones become uncomfortable when we outgrow them.
- We create self-imposed limitations when we are threatened by the prospect of change.
- When opportunity knocks we have to take the plunge or we will miss the boat.
- You can be all you want to be.

2

Decisions, Decisions, Decisions

'Even more than we are doers,
we are deciders. Once our decision
is clear the doing becomes effortless,
for then the universe supports and
empowers our action.'

RALPH BLUM

Even optimists get the blues! But the difference between an optimist and a pessimist lies in their reaction and attitude to challenging events. When things are looking bad the pessimist is having her own expectations fulfilled; she is part of her own self-fulfilling prophecy: I knew this good time couldn't last; I told you that plan was no good; it was bound to rain when I decided to go out for the day; how can you expect anyone to support you?; life is unfair; what with the state of the world, no wonder I'm always depressed ... etc., etc. Nevertheless, listen carefully, and behind the moans and groans you will hear a small note of triumph (you see I'm right again, life's a bitch): the pessimist wins the dubious victory of proving that she always loses and that she knew all along that she would. So there may be a strange reward that keeps the pessimist nicely victimized (and safe from having to take any positive action).

The optimist, facing the same situation that demoralized the pessimist, is different because she always has a coping strategy. When she goes down she doesn't escape the emotional pain but neither does it offer her attractions to stay in that low place: there is no wish fulfilment or sense of proving she is right. Optimists are positive thinkers who believe in the intrinsic goodness of the universe and its inhabitants, and they put their energy into fulfilling positive expectations. A positive mental approach is based on the principle that we have the power to change our own reality. This means that (even if disaster strikes), the optimist knows that 'This too will pass' and that she has the strength of character to survive. And for this approach to work she needs a plan. And to enact a plan she must first make some clear decisions.

When things just seem to happen to you

Sometimes our path gets very rocky. There are times when we feel as if we can't handle one more difficulty or disappointment, and then one more appears! The first skill we lose when we feel like this is the ability to trust our own judgement and decision-making powers. Self-doubt and insecurity flare up when we are under pressure, and with the carpet pulled out from under our feet it's hard to find a centred and grounded place to stand. Just at the point when we most need to make some decisions we find that it is the hardest thing in the world to do. Figure 2 shows how this lack of self-trust can create a self-perpetuating negative downward spiral.

One of the ways we can escape this 'things happen to me' spiral is by working directly on the decision-making process.

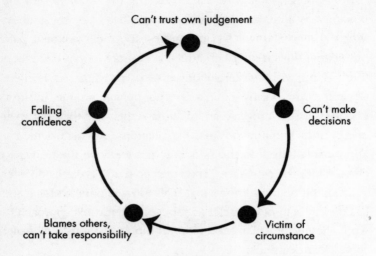

Figure 2: 'Things Happen to Me' Spiral

But you can't please all of the people all of the time

Life-changing decisions stir up the people who share your life, and often this is why pessimists remain in the 'safe' prison of their victim status. Change involves much more than a brainstorming session; it requires commitment and courage. At some point you have to stop asking for, and listening to, everyone else's opinion of what you should and shouldn't do and decide for yourself. You have to be prepared to put your needs first, and if you are over-concerned with pleasing others you will never get what you really want. Yes, it really is quite possible to be too nice, and if you think that you have never been too saccharine sweet for your own good then think again.

Use IDA

IDA is a simple formula that you can use whenever you are uncertain about what to decide and therefore how to act. IDA represents the following process:

Intention ➡ Decision ➡ Action

You can't act if you can't decide how to act, and you can't make a decision unless you know what you intend to happen. If action is the flower then intention is its seed, and as you define your intention so you define your action. Think of any area in your life where you would like to see changes.

Intention: Discover your intention. Ask yourself, 'What do I want to happen?' Be as specific as possible and write down your answers.

Decision: Clarify your decisions by asking yourself, 'How do I make it happen?' Brainstorm for ideas and write down everything that comes up, even if it seems irrelevant at the moment (new ideas often emerge with this technique).

Action: Life changes begin when you change yourself. If you keep on acting in the same way you will get the same result, and if this isn't what you want you must change your behaviour. Use assertive communication skills (positive and diplomatic) and go for your goal!

People-pleaser checklist

Answer the following questions to discover just how nice you are prepared to be.

1. Do you ever feel taken for granted?
2. Will you stay late at work when asked, even if you don't want to?
3. Do you ever ask permission to speak or to act in a certain way?
4. Do you often apologize for your behaviour?
5. Are you ever worried about what others think?
6. Do you ever think that some people are 'better' than you?
7. Do you often use the word 'sorry'?
8. Is it hard for you to say no to people?
9. Do you often find yourself doing things that you really don't want to do?
10. Do you ever not say what you really mean?

Whenever you feel your smile sticking to your face, whenever you are saying yes when you are longing to say no, whenever you are feeling used and are becoming resentful, whenever you feel angry with the world ... it's time to stop trying to please everyone else and time to start pleasing yourself.

Albert Einstein once said that the single most important decision any of us will ever make is whether or not to believe the universe is friendly. Make this decision in the affirmative: decide to become an optimist and use your strength of character to live the life that you deserve. Face your fears and stand up for yourself and you will always have a game plan to rely on when the going gets tough. You *can* change your reality if you decide to do so.

Reflections

- Pessimists never have to take any positive action (they can just play the victim).
- Optimists are positive thinkers who believe in the intrinsic goodness of the universe, and they put their energy into fulfilling positive expectations.
- Self-doubt and insecurity flare up when we are under pressure.
- Life changes begin when you change yourself.
- Are you being too nice for your own good?
- It's time to please yourself: decide to change.

3

Heaven Is Not a Place

'When you find happiness and contentment in being yourself, you have found heaven. It is time for mankind to awaken to its own brilliance of being.'

GRAHAM BISHOP

You won't find heaven nestled cosily amongst fluffy white clouds behind pearly gates, because heaven is not a place, it's a state of mind.

Life in the 21st century offers us glamorous images; fast food; items to take out, carry out and throw out ... we are bombarded with sensual delights and our appetite can become jaded. The 24-hour society will sell us anything at any time of the day or night, but we are discovering that convenience doesn't necessarily create happiness: you can have a refrigerator full of food, a wardrobe full of clothes and a house full of televisions and still feel discontented. Many of us have become brilliant jugglers: home, work, family, friends/home, work, family, friends ... it's a good act and it does mean that you get to hold *all* of the balls, but does it really mean that you get to *have it all?* And what does *having it all* actually mean to you?

Consider this: it is 7am. I get out of bed and the sun is shining. I am **pleased** and go for a shower, but there's no soap left and I'm **irritated.** I dress for my important meeting. I'm **delighted** with my new suit and fix breakfast. I accidentally pour milk down my skirt and am **horrified**. I change my clothes, rush to the car and the battery is flat. I'm **devastated** and phone for a taxi. The cab arrives in 5 minutes and I am **relieved**. The time is 7.35am. And I am **exhausted**! Riding an emotional roller coaster is absolutely shattering.

Modern life offers us a never-ending supply of things and ideas that excite our emotions and desires. We pay for this excitement with a compulsory roller coaster ride. Before we know it, we are off again: up and down, up and down, up and down …

The spiritual power within you

We spend our lives looking for happiness and contentment by striving to achieve success in the material world, believing that this is our only reality. Searching for fulfilment we try to find our satisfaction in external things: money, alcohol, career, relationships, food, sex, workouts, designer clothes … you name it! I don't need to tell you that this approach doesn't work. However gorgeous the man or woman, the shoes, the Belgian chocolates … they *cannot* do it for us (at least not for long). So, what exactly is it that is missing from these experiences?

Of course we are living in a physical world and we have material wants and needs, but we are also so much more. Between the emotional peaks and troughs lies another path that leads to a strong sense of inner awareness, trust, creativity and intuition. This is where we discover the peace and serenity of our own spirituality. When you find yourself having that 'there must be more to life than this' feeling, you are right: what you see with your eyes is not all that you get.

We understand and interpret our lives through the energies of our minds, bodies, spirits and emotions. For example, our **mind** creates **mental energy,** which gives us the experience of **thinking.** The table below shows how each of our faculties creates a different kind of energy and provides a different element of our total experience.

	Type of energy	**Experience**
Mind	Mental	Thinking
Body	Physical	Doing
Emotions	Emotional	Feeling
Spirit	Spiritual	Connecting

We are all pretty good at **thinking**, having been taught by a society that elevates the importance of the mind. **Doing** is also something we know a lot about: we can run about moving stuff around the universe all day! Our ability to know and express our **feelings** is sometimes a bit trickier because we have a lot of mixed up ideas about our emotions (for example we might believe that showing our feelings is a weakness or we might hide emotions which we think we 'shouldn't' be feeling). And as for **connecting** with our spirituality, well, this is certainly not something we were instructed in at school.

A total experience

For a total experience we need to bring our whole self to each moment of our life: this means using our mind, body, spirit and emotions. To demonstrate this, just choose a recent incident in your life and reflect on the way you understood what was happening at the time.

What were your thoughts?	(mind)
What did you do?	(body)
What were your feelings?	(emotions)
How did you connect?	(spirit)

You can probably answer the first three questions quite easily, but could you answer the last one? Do you know how to connect with your spiritual energy? Do you know what this feels like?

Your spiritual energy

A client once told me that she couldn't describe herself as a spiritual person because she wasn't religious. But the reality and experience of our spirituality is not dependent on a particular religion or a belief in God: we connect with our spiritual energy when we get in touch with that part of ourselves that is joined to the energy of universe. Think of a time when you had a strong gut feeling about something and you were proved right; this is an example of connecting. What about that uplifting experience you had listening to a piece of music, enjoying sex, out in the garden in the sun, holding a new born baby? ... Whenever something takes you out of yourself in some way, you are being lifted beyond your physical experience, because your spirit is connecting with universal energy. We feel this connection as a sense of oneness with the rest of the universe. And when we become aware of this as our spiritual energy we begin to understand the meaning and purpose of the events and circumstances of our lives. Without awareness of our spirit we can only think, feel and act, and so we cannot connect with the larger picture.

Some people believe in God and to these people God is understood as universal energy. There are many others who have no concept of God and are more comfortable with abstractions such as higher power, divinity, inner guidance, Higher Self, cosmic power, spirit, the universe or whatever other preference. Don't let your mind tie you in knots over which concepts you can accept and which you can't. You will experience your spirituality in a unique and personal way and you will *feel* the spiritual power within you (it is beyond logic and reason and name). So rise above any mental conflict and allow yourself to transcend conceptual reality (suspend disbelief for a while). Let yourself to be taken on a wonderful, uplifting and inspiring spiritual journey of amazing self-discovery and grace to awaken to your own 'brilliance of being'.

Reflections

- There is another path that you can take, and it lies between your exhausting emotional highs and lows.
- We are expert thinkers and doers but we also need to develop our emotional and spiritual aspects.
- Do you know what it feels like to connect with your spiritual energy?
- Your sense of the spiritual does not depend on religious beliefs; your spirituality lies within *you*.
- When you connect with your spirituality you are able to see the meaning and purpose in your life.
- Open up to your spiritual energy and awaken to your own brilliance of being!

4

You Have the Power

*'Take your life in your own hands,
and what happens? A terrible thing: no
one to blame.'*

Erica Jong

Decades fly by, a lifetime may pass, and still we may not get it! If we are looking back in anger and pointing the finger of blame at anyone for anything that has happened to us, we haven't understood a most important principle: we own our lives; they are ours to live and we choose what to make of them. The acceptance of this responsibility does not always feel joyful and liberating. When things go wrong, relationships flounder, tragedy strikes, or even if we are just having a bad day, who of us doesn't look around for someone, something, anything to blame? And passing the buck does provide an immediate relief (lessens the intensity of our emotions and takes the pressure off momentarily), and maybe someone has done you wrong, but then what? The joy of blame is very short lived and it takes us into a cul de sac of emotions; it doesn't lead us out to anywhere new, and we can only keep going round in the same circle.

Well it must be my fault, then

Do you recognize this one? *If he/she isn't to blame then I have created this situation; it's all my responsibility and it must be my fault. If I attract what I radiate, get what I expect, can draw negativity into my life, can even make myself ill with worrying and stressful thoughts, then my life is a mess because I am not positive enough/spiritual enough/balanced enough ...*

Guilt and blame are always hanging around, ready to be used whenever things aren't so clear. 'He left me; what did I do wrong?' 'The children are out of control; I must be a bad parent.' Whether we blame someone else or ourselves, we remain a victim. Self-empowerment comes when we can step out of all blame and guilt and view our circumstances with a degree of objectivity. Stop getting so up-close and personal about everything and look at what is really going on, energetically speaking.

EXERCISE:

Are you giving your power away?

Sit quietly for a few moments. Close your eyes and imagine yourself full of vibrant and dynamic energy. Feel the power within you and then feel yourself sending this force out into the world.

Yes, you really are a powerhouse of amazing energy; how are you using this resource? We can give away our power in many ways. The following list identifies some ways in which we might be doing this.

1. Recognizing a problem and blaming someone else (now we have to wait for them to do something about it).

2. Blaming ourselves (losing self-respect and confidence).

3. Waiting for someone to change (we will quite possibly be waiting forever).

4. Looking to the past with regret and blame (and losing the ability to act in the present).

5. Looking to the future in fear (and becoming too afraid to act now).

6. Waiting for something to change (being passive and reactive).

Each time we try to find the solutions to our problems by looking outside ourselves for answers we allow our energy to leak away.

Your life in your hands

The only way to change your circumstances is to change yourself, and you have been born with the capacity to do this: use this ability. When life throws us a challenge we have three choices:

1. Dive for cover and look for a scapegoat.
2. Become the scapegoat.
3. Respond creatively.

Looking for and being the scapegoat are the choices of the victim (likes to be a martyr, feels undeserving, has low self-worth, doesn't want any responsibility, can always blame others, is afraid to rock the boat, never has to take a risk). Responding creatively is the choice of someone who knows they have the power to make positive changes. This response is not always easy and it requires courage and tenacity at a time when things might be very difficult. But what else have we to do in this life if not to take responsibility for ourselves and the way that we live? Surely there can be no other reason for us to be here.

Victim consciousness is always linked with low self-esteem.

How can we continue to let ourselves lose out, miss out, get treated like a doormat, be abused and the rest unless we believe that we deserve to be treated in this way? When you next find yourself diving for cover or flirting dangerously with guilt and blame, ask yourself these questions: Where is my self-respect? What do I deserve? Am I a person with integrity? How can I stand up for myself? Am I taking responsibility for my life?

10 ways to keep your power

1. Decide to take charge of your life.
2. Know that your heart is strong; you will survive your emotional peaks and troughs.
3. Believe in your own power (never give it away).
4. Do what you have to do to get your life in order.
5. Let your creative energy guide you (you do know what to do and how to do it).
6. Tell the truth (to others and to yourself).
7. Get your head out of the sand and look things in the eye.
8. Trust your intuition and your heart; never betray your deepest feelings.
9. Be ready to follow things through (let your inspirations become your reality).
10. Never hook into guilt and blame (visualize them floating away in a bubble of light).

Reflections

- Self-empowerment comes when we step out of blame and guilt.
- Every time we look outside ourselves for answers we allow our energy to leak away.
- If you are waiting for someone to change you will probably be waiting forever.
- You have the courage and tenacity to respond creatively.
- How can we let ourselves be victimized unless we believe we deserve to be treated badly?
- Never let yourself down.

Falling In and Out of Love

'If you are loving the wrong person, loving the right way won't make any difference.'

BARBARA DE ANGELIS

Why do we make so many mistakes in the love department? How come we start so dreamy and starry-eyed about our latest love interest and so often end up with a severe case of disillusionment?

The romantic within us is a sucker for what I call the 'Love Myths'. These are mistaken beliefs about the nature of true love that lead us into making poor relationship choices over and over again. If your relationships are a disaster zone you may recognize some of the following scenarios:

- If a partner is too nice you get bored.
- You just knew she was the one for you the moment you met.
- He finds it hard to express his emotions and so you need to give him your emotional support at all times.
- To feel truly in love you need drama and excitement.
- When the sex is great you know it's love.

- You stay a long time in a relationship which demoralizes you because you think everything is your fault.
- The relationship is poor but you know he loves you really deep down because he is so full of remorse after he has treated you badly.
- You love to be in love and need to feel ecstatic in order to stay in a relationship.
- You put your partner on a pedestal and when she falls off you are disappointed in her.

Love Myths send us on a never-ending search for *the one* – the Prince or Princess Charming who we know is out there waiting for us, our perfect partner who we will recognize immediately as the one whom will fulfil our every need. Such is life in the movies, romantic fiction and many popular love songs, but this is not how it works in reality! If we have such expectations of our partner, we are misunderstanding the nature of true intimacy and are doomed to make unsatisfactory relationships.

Are you a love junkie?

Scientists have discovered that the high we get from falling in love comes from a chemical called phenylethylamine (PEA), which is manufactured in our bodies when we first feel the physical sensation of romantic love. We all know how this feels: we fall in love and the world is full of birdsong and promise; everything is possible and life looks clearer and brighter as we look at it through the eyes of love.

Romance is an important part of an intimate relationship, but it cannot exist alone, and if we need this constant high to convince us that we are 'in love' then our relationships will always be short-lived. How many times have you felt disappointed by the ordinary, domestic parts of your relationships?

When you are putting out the rubbish or cleaning the toilet you need more than that initial rush of PEA to sustain you year after year. A long-term commitment (that works) requires an understanding of the dynamics of intimate relationships – but even this won't work if you are loving the wrong person.

What's in your Lovemap?

We manufacture the love drug PEA in response to certain stimuli that turn us on at the deepest level. When we are very young we subconsciously absorb and retain any experiences of pain and pleasure that make a powerful impression on us; this process is referred to as sexual imprinting. Dr John Money, a renowned sexologist, has created the concept of Lovemaps to describe this imprinting. We all have a Lovemap that contains both the positive and negative imprinting that causes us to be sexually attracted to other people.

This then explains the excitement and yet helplessness that we feel when we first fall in love; it's almost as if we have no choice in the matter:

when I first saw him I adored his floppy brown fringe and I had to get to know him; she danced like a dream and I couldn't stop thinking about her; he was so intense and quiet, I just had to discover those hidden depths; she was so small and defenceless looking, I felt that all I wanted to do was to protect her forever.

Yes, a floppy fringe might be all it takes to send us into full-blown madness at the sight of a stranger; it has been said that we spend more time and care in buying a new video than we do on evaluating a new love interest.

You are really at the mercy of your sexual imprinting until you check out the contents of your personal Lovemap. Answer the

following questions to see which characteristics make you go
weak at the knees.

My Lovemap

1. What physical features do you usually fall for?

2. What type of person most attracts you?

3. Which qualities do your past lovers share (negative as well as
positive)?

4. Would you say that you always go for the same type?

5. Does this type suit you?

6. Do relationships with your preferred type often end in tears?

Are you loving the wrong person?

Perhaps your favourite teacher had red hair and now you are
besotted by every redhead. Your father may be a talented
musician and so you find yourself attracted to musical men.
These positive imprintings are quite easy to recognize and in
themselves create no problems unless these features are the
only ones holding the relationship together.

But Lovemaps can also be negative, and this is why we so
often find ourselves making poor relationship decisions. Led by
our sexual imprinting we can find ourselves in inappropriate
relationships time and time again. Indeed, we can even find
ourselves addicted to people with behaviour patterns that are
non-supportive, critical or abusive. For example, if your father
was emotionally withdrawn when you were a little girl you may
well be inclined to seek relationships with cold, unemotional

men (repeating a familiar pattern and also giving you the chance at last to change the pattern). Or maybe you watched your mother have affairs and now you can't ever trust a woman long enough to sustain true intimacy?

Get to grips with your Lovemap and look particularly closely at any repeating patterns within your relationships. If you are relying on your girlfriend's dancing talents to see you through the hard times you must know that such external attractions are not enough on their own. And if you find yourself caught in a compulsive attraction for the wrong type of person it is time to realize that you are stuck in a relationship that will never lead anywhere, however much love you pour into it.

Stop blaming your inadequate partner and turn the focus back on yourself. Why have you attracted this relationship? Investigate the contents of your Lovemap and break the attraction traps that cause you pain. Remind yourself that you deserve loving and supportive relationships and that you will attract whatever you think that you deserve. You can choose who to love.

Reflections

- If you are loving the wrong person, no amount of love will make any difference.
- Romance is an important part of our relationships but it cannot exist alone: the effects of the love drug will eventually wear off.
- Led by our sexual imprinting we can find ourselves in inappropriate relationships again and again.
- Stop blaming an inadequate partner and turn the focus back on yourself.
- Why have you attracted this relationship?
- You can choose who to love.

6

The Web of Life

*'This we know: all things are
connected like the blood that unites
one family. All things are connected.*

*'Whatever befalls the earth befalls the
sons of earth. Man did not weave the
web of life. He is merely a strand on it.
Whatever he does to the web he does to
himself.'*

CHIEF SEATTLE

We are the universe: we are made of it and it is made of us. We
are made of the same stuff. The universe is pure energy and this
energy creates all the structures and forms that go to form our
reality. Look around you and you will see objects that appear to
be totally separate and unlike each other. But the basic building
blocks of your chair, your cup of tea and you are the same.

Everything is connected and whatever you say and do, and
even whatever you believe and think, will have an effect on the
rest of the universe. Hard to believe? Modern physicists are
beginning to discover that Western science and Eastern mysti-
cism share a similar vision. In scientific as well as mystical

thought we are indeed all connected: we share universal energy; we *are* universal energy. There is only one world, with two aspects: the visible and the invisible. Everything that exists contains the spark of universal consciousness (divinity, spirit or whatever word you like to use). When we can acknowledge the interconnectedness of all things and people we begin our spiritual journey. When we understand that we share this eternal spark with every other creature in the universe (and that includes our very worst enemy) we know it is time to go beyond the visible realms to examine our true spiritual nature.

It is easy to understand the theory behind the words and so much harder to feel the experience. At this point I would ask you to forget about the proof of our links with every thing, everyone and every part of the universe. Let go of mental analysis and open up to your inner awareness. If you feel that you don't know how to do this, just relax; believe me, you have done this countless times. Your spirit has been busy every moment of your life. It has been bringing insights, giving you ideas, encouraging your creativity and opening your heart; you just haven't been aware of the source of these gifts. Suspend all disbelief and trust your own experience as you do the following exercise.

EXERCISE:

We are all connected

As our spiritual awareness develops we can go beyond the scientific explanation of how we are all part of the same whole. As we tune in to our inner senses we begin to experience the connections: feelings of separation fall away and we know for sure that we are part of something so much larger than ourselves. I once heard someone explain the illusion of our separateness from each other by comparing us with trees. All trees appear to stand alone, although their leaves may whisper to each other and their branches may touch in the gentle breezes. But despite the fact that all trees appear to be separate, deep in the earth their roots are often intertwined with each other. And the earth unites them all. What a beautiful image this is!

Sit somewhere quietly and contemplate this image. If you can go outside and see real trees, all the better. Look at these trees (real or imagined) and see the way they stand so proud and upward-reaching and seemingly so alone. Now become aware of their strong roots, which depend upon the earth for their nourishment. Visualize the interlocking root systems beneath the soil. As your trees rustle in the breeze, recognize that although they stand alone they are deeply connected. In just such a way we too are united in the material/spiritual universe. Think about this image throughout the day.

Connecting from your heart centre

OK, so we know that we share a divine spark with everyone and when life is swinging along beautifully who could deny this truth? But what about the days when your half-full cup looks half-empty and there's no magic anywhere? Sometimes we just don't like ourselves and don't like anyone else either: when negativity strikes it feels as if our divine spark has been snuffed out. It hasn't of course: your beautiful soul is still shining brightly and so is everyone else's. Negativity closes down our true perceptions as we retreat behind our defences; hearts close and minds go into overdrive. How can I feel divinely connected even to my best friend on such a day, let alone my worst enemy?

Sit quietly and relax. Close your eyes and visualize a big golden sunflower in the centre of your chest (your heart centre). If you think you can't visualize it, just know that it's there. Take your giant sunflower with you wherever you go, and be aware that it is blooming happily and beautifully. When you meet someone else see their sunflower too, and if you are having a communication problem with this person just relate to their sunflower. As you start coming from your heart centre you will feel others responding with more warmth. When life feels less than amazing, have a giant sunflower day and feel the difference.

You can use this technique whenever you are having a relationship problem: it's much easier to see the sunflowers than it is to feel frustrated and angry. When a client questioned this approach because she felt she would just be denying her feelings, I suggested that she give it a go to see what would happen. She used it with her ex-husband when they were discussing the holiday arrangements for their small daughter (always a sensitive subject). She was surprised by the effect: 'The sunflowers saved me. I was so much more centred and I was able to listen to his point of view instead of flying off the handle. I think he was amazed that I was so calm and approachable, and, you know, he even backed down over something that had really been annoying me.'

When we transcend our mind we open to a whole new set of possibilities. Have a happy sunflower day!

Learning to connect with our spiritual energy is an ongoing process; there are always new facets to see and experience. As we develop our self-awareness more and more, it becomes easier to make the connection. At first it may seem a little strained and forced and you may feel full of doubts about what you are or are not sensing. Take it slowly and don't take it too seriously – remember that laughter comes from the spirit. Try not to analyze your spiritual experiences; just feel them and value them. *The more you can appreciate them, the quicker you will develop.*

Reflections

- When we can acknowledge the interconnectedness of all things, we begin our spiritual journey.
- Your spirit has been active every moment of your life, bringing amazing gifts; just recognize this!
- The divine spark is within you; know that this is true.
- Transcend your mind and everything becomes possible.
- Appreciate greatly and the rewards will be far beyond your expectations.
- Your spiritual journey has begun.

7

Everywhere You Go, There You Are!

'Do I have the personal qualities it takes to succeed? This is the most important question of all.'

PETER LYNCH

Being yourself may not always sound an attractive goal. Sometimes when things don't look so great we may start wishing that we were someone else or somewhere else! *If only I could get away from here; if only I had another job; if only I could meet a new lover; if only I had more money; if only I was more like* ... Yes, the grass may look greener on the other side, but when you eventually get there you discover an obvious but amazing truth: you have taken yourself with you! There is no escaping yourself; changing your circumstances will not necessarily make you happier. Contentment begins with self-awareness and self-acceptance and it focuses on the now. While you are wishing that things could be different, you will always feel dissatisfied with what you have and who you are at this moment. The trick is to be able to accept yourself just as you are (including all the bits you don't like very much). When you are feeling more comfortable with who you are you gain a sense of inner peace and you take that with you wherever you go.

Success can be measured in many ways, but we cannot define it by external criteria alone: in other words, fame and fortune cannot necessarily 'fix' us. And I'm not advocating a life of obscurity and poverty because that won't fix us either. No, true success is felt inside: it's an inner sense of satisfaction about a job well done, an opportunity grasped, an outcome achieved, a problem resolved, and it always brings with it an underlying feeling of appreciation and well-being.

Your personal qualities

Tennis star Billie Jean King once said: 'Self-awareness is probably the most important thing towards becoming a champion.' I would take this even further and say that self-awareness is the key to a successful life. You take yourself wherever you go; you live with yourself every moment of your life; you cannot escape who you are; your relationship with yourself is the most significant and important relationship you will ever have. So get to know yourself!

You have the personal qualities it takes to succeed. There is no doubt about this, although you may be feeling unsure. You are strong, powerful, aware, resolute, determined and creatively inspired to live a fabulous life. Believe this to be true, because it is. Believe it to be true even when you don't believe it! In other words, when you are full of doubt and uncertainty remind yourself of who you really are: you are bigger than your negative thoughts and more powerful than your disbelief.

Learning to live with yourself

It's hard to live with someone who is unforgiving, treats you badly and criticizes you. If you are having an intimate relationship with someone like this then you will be feeling low in self-esteem and high in negativity and self-critical thoughts. But what is it like for you to live with yourself? We can be unbelievably hard on ourselves, can't we? Just when we need some support and kindness we often generate its opposite: we become our own worst critic (unforgiving, intolerant and unkind). Self-criticism is a fast track to negativity, depression and dissatisfaction; don't take this route. When the chips are down search for some self-compassion, look for self-forgiveness, give yourself some tender loving care. Don't think that you are all alone with your negative self-beliefs. We all find it hard to become the person we would most like to live with. But practice makes perfect and you can start right now.

Forgive yourself

So you have nasty thoughts and feel uncomfortable emotions; so do we all. Unless you are a saint you will share the whole range of human emotional responses, and this is quite natural. The next time you feel an uncomfortable emotion (such as jealousy, anger, shame or grief) don't compound it with guilt (because you 'shouldn't' be feeling it). If you feel it, then you feel it. Accept it and then it will pass; tie it up with guilt and you will stay locked within its jaws. Start to notice when these 'unacceptable' emotions emerge and acknowledge and release them. This practice will start to bring great personal benefits. Try the next exercise, which will help to get rid of some more personal demons.

Letting your skeletons out of the closet

We have all been wicked; we have all done and said things that we regret; we all make mistakes. We can never fully appreciate the wonder of life if we are tied up in memories of the past, and sometimes people spend their whole lives punishing themselves for something that happened long ago. If you have any shameful secrets hidden away, you will be feeling guilty and also fearful (that they may be revealed). Let your skeletons out of the closet.

- Invite each one out.

- Assess each one objectively.

- Remedy anything that you can.

- Let each one rattle off in peace.

As you bring your secrets out from the darkness of the closet and into the light of the day, they will lose their mystery and their powerful hold over you. Yes, you did that and you've paid your price in guilt and shame. And yes, you said that and its effect was disastrous. Perhaps you can apologize to someone or maybe you can just let it go. You have punished yourself enough so lighten up and move on.

Being yourself

Being yourself is the only way to happiness. There is no one else you can be. You may try to copy others or to be what they want you to be, but this will never work. If you are not being true to yourself you will become unhappy, depressed and angry. Your true self will emerge because this is who you really are. When you can accept yourself with the compassion that you deserve, your life will really start to take off. Self-tolerance makes you tolerant of others; self-compassion opens your heart; self-forgiveness allows you to let others off the hook. And when you change the way you feel about yourself on the inside, you attract different experiences on the outside. Be the positive, resourceful and creative person that you were meant to be and you will attract a powerful energetic response from the rest of the universe. Wherever you go you are bound to take yourself, so let that self be the best it can be. Let your constant companion be kind, supportive and nurturing and allow your life to become easy, peaceful, happy and satisfying.

Reflections

- There is no escaping yourself.
- Contentment begins with self-awareness and self-acceptance and it focuses on the now.
- True success is felt inside and it always brings an underlying feeling of appreciation and well-being.
- Self-awareness is the key to a successful life.
- Your relationship with yourself is the most significant and important relationship you will ever have.
- You have the personal qualities that it takes to succeed.

8

Don't Worry, Be Happy

'Maybe we cannot escape from the destiny of the human, but we have a choice: to suffer our destiny or to enjoy our destiny. To suffer, or to love and be happy.'

DON MIGUEL RUIZ

Don't worry, be happy. I know, it's easy to say and not quite so easy to do, isn't it? But – can you believe it? – scientists have discovered yet another syndrome for us to worry about? It's called GAD – Generalized Anxiety Disorder. So if we don't suffer from SAD (Seasonal Affective Disorder) we can still be well down in the dumps by embracing GAD. Frankly, I'd rather embrace happiness and feel GLAD to do so. I'm not being frivolous about your worries and concerns; I do appreciate just how hard life can often be. But we need to demystify this GAD syndrome: it's no new and terrible disease, just a fancy new spin on overactive worrying. The great news is, we can easily learn to stop fretting and obsessing about our problems, *if we want to.*

Choosing to be glad

You can choose your view of the world: your cake can be half eaten or you can have half left; you can make things happen or have things happen to you; you can think worrying thoughts every waking moment of your day or you can fill your mind with more pleasant things. Yes, you really do have this choice. Of course, it's no good just ignoring your difficulties and pretending your problems will go away: if things need tackling then sort them out. Act rather than worry: if it's possible, *do* something to relieve your anxieties (sometimes we worry because we are afraid to take action). And if there is absolutely nothing you can do to change the situation, what is the point of worrying? You will only get into GAD, which you know will just take you lower and lower into the realms of depression. Who needs this? The scientists say that GAD (or excessive worrying) affects more than 2 million people in the UK and it affects more women than men.

It's time to ensure that you are not part of this particular statistic. Stress is a happiness buster as well as a health hazard, relationship annihilator and total life destroyer. Yes, choose to be glad and choose to let go of unnecessary worrying (stress) – the rest of your life is at stake!

Just thinking about stress is enough to make us tense

Well, it's true, isn't it? Newspapers and magazines are forever telling us that 'stress kills' and feed us with frightening statistics that prove that stress is the main cause of terrifying illnesses. A huge stress reduction industry has sprung up, providing books, therapies, courses, relaxation classes, fitness centres ... all to help us de-stress. Let's lighten up and stop blaming stress for all our worries, as if it's an illness with a cure. There's no need to be afraid of becoming stressed (and so making ourselves more stressed). *Stress is only a word that is used to describe the feelings we have when we are not coping very well with our lives.*

This definition helps us to get a grip on the concept of stress. How often have you felt uptight and out of control and told yourself that you are 'just feeling stressed'? But this only ever serves to add to your anxiety, doesn't it? It doesn't address the underlying problem and it offers no hope of a solution.

E X E R C I S E :

Getting it together – an action plan

The next time you think you are suffering from stress do the following:

Step 1 Stop worrying about what stress will do to you. Recognize that you are only experiencing a feeling of being unable to cope (believe it or not, we all feel like this some of the time).

Step 2 Look at the situation and ask yourself why you can't cope.

Step 3 Ask yourself if you can do anything to resolve the situation. If you can't, then accept this and let go of the worry. If you can, then make an action plan.

Step 4 Discover what needs doing. Make a list of the practical steps you need to take. Then ACT! Take each step as it comes and work your way through this dilemma. You will feel more and more fantastic as you start to deal with your own difficulties.

Forget worrying about your stress levels and just do what needs to be done. You have all the ability you need to cope with whatever life throws at you: you can find your own solutions to all your problems.

Money can't buy it

While we look to the material world to fulfil all our needs we will never be truly happy. Once we are adequately fed, clothed and sheltered we must look beyond the 'things' of the world if we are to be truly happy and content (more clothes, more food, a bigger house will not do it for us). It is so easy to become distracted by the bright lights and glittering prizes: who hasn't longed for that special something, only to find that it brought a short-lived pleasure? We are looking for much more than material gifts. We need spiritual and emotional fulfilment, to feel a sense of connection with each other and with the natural world, to have an underlying sense of meaning and purpose to our days, and to feel deep appreciation for the miracle which is our life. We are bigger than our worries and we don't have to succumb to them; we only need to look inside ourselves to discover the happiness we seek.

A day of peace and tranquillity

Give up the worrying habit and decide to take the lighter path today. Wake up and appreciate yourself. Sing in the shower and uplift your spirits. Speak with an encouraging voice and don't criticize others. Remember to smile as much as you can (this will make you and everyone around you feel much better). Keep up this level of positive energy and you will notice that others will be more responsive than usual. Let yourself be yourself and say what you are feeling and thinking. Trust your own judgements and decisions and follow through with appropriate action.

Today you have lifted your energy into a positive cycle and in doing so have created new choices for yourself. How does it feel? Why not choose to enjoy your destiny every day?

Reflections

- We can stop obsessing about our problems if we want to.
- Choose to be glad.
- Just thinking about stress is enough to make us tense.
- Stress is only a word that is used to describe the feelings we have when we are not coping very well.
- You can find your own solutions to all your problems.
- Look inside yourself to discover the happiness you seek.

9

Becoming Your Higher Self

'Spiritual growth comes from increasing contact with your Higher Self and allowing it to become the director of every part of your life. Once you begin a path of spiritual growth – seeking, learning, exploring the greater being that you are, and uncovering the mysteries of the universe – you will never be the same.'

SANAYA ROMAN

The truth is that once we experience the need for 'something more' in our lives, we become irresistibly drawn to our own spirituality; nothing else can quench that extraordinary thirst.

Where is your Higher Self?

We understand and interpret our lives through our mind, body, spirit and emotions. Our mental, physical, spiritual and emotional energies are subtle, interwoven and mutually dependent, and when these energies are flowing smoothly and harmoniously our experience is complete and we feel balanced, in control, aware and really in touch with what is going on. If there is an imbalance anywhere within our energy systems we will feel unconnected, out of synch, low in confidence, unsure and uneasy.

Our **BODY**	gives us the	**PHYSICAL**	experience of	**DOING**
Our **MIND**	gives us the	**MENTAL**	experience of	**THINKING**
Our **EMOTIONS**	give us the	**EMOTIONAL**	experience of	**FEELING**
Our **SPIRIT**	gives us the	**SPIRITUAL**	experience of	**CONNECTING**

Our energies are interdependent: they flow freely amongst themselves, colouring, shaping and changing each other. For example, how we feel affects what we do: change the emotion and our actions may change. When we learn to recognize and use our spiritual energy this will have an amazing impact on our doing, thinking and feeling. When we connect with our spirituality we do it via the very highest part of ourselves, which we call our Higher Self.

Figure 3 is a diagrammatic representation of an individual's energy systems. The outer circumference represents the ending of the person and the beginning of the rest of the world. Although we know that our energies are never static and are interlinked, the diagram places **physical** energy at the outermost perimeter. This is because *doing* is always our most obvious response and it is outer-directed. The following circle represents **mental** energy, because *thinking* is a more internal activity. The circle after that represents **emotional** energy, as *feeling* is an even more inner-directed experience. Next we touch our **spiritual** energy, which gives us that feeling of *connecting* with the life force, and we do this through our inner awareness. At the very centre of ourselves, within our spiritual

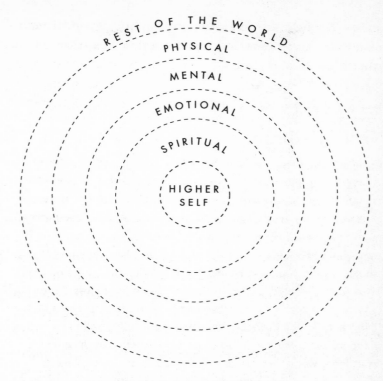

Figure 3: An Individual's Energy System

energy, we see the jewel of our **Higher Self**, shining brightly and illuminating everything. Remember that this diagram is only intended to *represent* your energy; please don't get into conceptual difficulties by trying to understand what it all means.

Discovering your Higher Self

There is a strong sense that the journey to our Higher Self leads away from the physical body and outer-directed activities, beyond the realms of our mind and emotions into a sacred space deep within. Some of you will recognize this sense of *going into* yourself, but for others this idea will be difficult to grasp. The only way to experience this is to experience it! In other words, you can't understand it with words alone. So put your book down and relax.

EXERCISE:

Going within

Sit quietly and comfortably. Close your eyes and keep them closed for 10 minutes.

What did you experience?

If you are used to relaxation techniques or have meditated, you may have been able to drift off nicely into another state of awareness. For others this little exercise may have been a bit of a shock. Would you have believed that there's so much going on in there? Mind chatter, bodily discomforts, external noises distracting you, more mental chitchat. If you have never done this kind of thing before, you probably only managed to stay within for two or three minutes. Relax – this exercise was only to introduce you to your inner world. Your Higher Self is there, amongst all those distractions: look at Figure 3 again and see how your jewel sits at the centre of your being.

Over the next few days allow yourself to become aware of your spiritual centre. Whenever you think about your Higher Self you could visualize a bright, shining, precious jewel of your choice, blazing brightly within you. Visualizing only means imagining, and if that's hard, then just knowing it's there is enough.

The spiritual world speaks to us through intuition and imagination: these are the voices of the spirit. Many of us have forgotten our intuitive and imaginative gifts. As the wonder years of early childhood pass away, the world loses its glory and freshness – we are so busy trying to 'grow up' and 'fit in'. As we learn to put away childish things, our imagination and intuition often get buried in the dressing-up clothes box.

I remember a time when I was about seven years old and I put on my fairy gear – long dress, big shoes with heels (my mother's), trailing chiffon scarves – and went down the garden to fairyland. But when I got there I could only see a fence, a tree, some grass: my magic place had gone! My fairy dress just couldn't do it for me any more and it felt like such a loss. I have spent the last 43 years searching for that wonder, magic and excitement, only to find that it hasn't gone anywhere; it was just buried deeply inside me.

When you allow your imagination some freedom and start to trust your intuition, your whole world will respond, so why not hitch your wagon to a star and come along for the ride?

Reflections

- Your Higher Self is your point of contact with the spiritual world.
- As soon as you recognize and start to use your spiritual energy, you will never be the same!
- Visualize the jewel at your spiritual core. See it shining and know that it is illuminating you.
- Wonder, magic and excitement didn't get thrown out with your toys: you can find these feelings again.
- Belief is strong magic, so hitch your wagon to a star and start to believe in your dreams.
- You deserve to reach your full potential, so let your Higher Self show you the way.

10
Relax and Take Control

'We have become so accustomed to crisis and deadlines that we feel almost lost if we are not putting out some kind of fire. In fact, if we really were honest, there is something dramatic and exciting about handling a crisis. It makes us feel as if we have some modicum of control in our lives.'

ANNE WILSON SCHAEF

The concepts of relaxation and control are strange bedfellows. How can we successfully fight all those fires if we loosen up, let go and unwind? And when our days are a chaotic muddle from the moment we wake up to the moment we collapse into bed, we may begin to think that life is just a never-ending obstacle course. But it doesn't have to be (unless that's the way you like it).

If we are addicted to drama, crises and adrenaline, we will know only too well those twin emotions: exhilaration and exhaustion. Lurching from one scenario to another in an effort to allay potential disasters and calamities may help us to feel in control but ultimately it is a tiring and unrewarding business.

Out of control and in a panic

When we are not sure of where we are going and why, we often panic and create diversions where we can demonstrate control. This is quite easy to do and it works in the very short term. For example, imagine having a disagreement with your partner; instead of expressing your real feelings you suddenly remember a piece of work that must be done immediately. You rush off in a fever of activity to show yourself that you can at least accomplish something (all the while denying your emotions and hiding them away inside). 'Do-aholism' keeps us nice and busy when we don't want to face our feelings.

But denial is like a huge hungry monster that keeps making an appearance when we least expect it: suddenly we are unaccountably angry/depressed/frightened (as our denied emotions resurface) and we feel out of control and in a panic. We can keep the monster quiet by creating yet another distraction (a problem that must be solved) or we can stop and listen to what it has to say.

Real control brings peace and harmony

You need never be afraid of your feelings; they are a natural part of you and will only hurt you if you ignore them and refuse to accept them. Emotions express our real needs in a very clear and straightforward way: you can always know your deepest desires because you can always feel them at some level. Denial inevitably causes pain (emotional and physical) and it has nothing to do with really being in control.

Real control is all about being balanced: when we are feeling creative and spontaneous and full of life our energy is naturally controlled and harmonious. So you can take charge of your life, but only if you are ready to make a truthful assessment of where you are and where you really want to be (no denials, no beating about the bush, no procrastination, only honesty). Try the following exercise to discover if there are any areas of your life that feel out of balance.

EXERCISE:

Life zone checklist

Relationships
Are your relationships good for you?
Do you ever feel taken for granted by your family/friends/partner?

Self-Image
Are you positive and upbeat?
Do you believe in yourself?
Are you self-confident?

Health and Fitness:
Does your lifestyle support good health?
Are you getting enough exercise?
Do you look after yourself?
Are you high in body confidence?

Money
Are you good at managing your money?
Do you ever spend more than you earn?
Do you need to earn more money?

Work
Do you like the work that you do?
Is your job fulfilling?
Would you like a career change?

Spirituality
Are you able to switch off from doing and just be?
Can you tap into your inner strength?
Do you believe that your contribution is important?

What do your answers reveal? Are there any areas of your life that feel out of synch?

Taking charge

We only really feel in control of our lives when we can recognize that we help to create 'what happens to us' and that we do this with a combination of our beliefs, expectations and behaviour. But why would we help to create a difficult relationship, loss of confidence or unhappy work conditions, for example?

Because discontent is a sign that we are not running at full potential, it can be very useful to examine our dissatisfactions and trace them back to their beginnings. When and why did this relationship start becoming problematic? Has it always been like this and is it only now that I can see it? Why is my confidence so low? What are my self-beliefs? Do I let people treat me badly? How long have I been fed up at work? Is it time for a career change?

It's always very hard to accept creative responsibility for our discontent and much easier (in the short term) to lay the blame elsewhere. But each time we blame someone or something for our situation we are giving away our power. How can we change anything if it's all someone else's fault? We can only wait for them to alter their behaviour; are you waiting for someone to change?

Taking control of your life means making the most of your life. You are not a victim of circumstance or of any person; you have the power to create the life you want. Accept accountability for your thoughts, feelings and actions, because they create your future. Change may be frightening, but no-change can be a much more terrifying prospect!

10 easy ways to change and take control

1. Decide what you want to change and how you can take the first step.
2. Take the first step!
3. Believe in yourself and know that you deserve the best in life.
4. Keep positive and stay away from negative people who will only bring you down.
5. If you feel afraid to change (what will people think? ... what if it all goes wrong? ... can I do this?) just face your fears and do it anyway.
6. Recognize and respect your feelings; they demonstrate your real needs.
7. Visualize the change you are looking for. See your successful outcome in your mind's eye and really know that it will happen.
8. You teach other people how to treat you. This means that if you let them treat you badly they will carry on doing so. Teach them to treat you well.
9. Speak up and say what you mean. You will never get what you want if you can't ask for it.
10. Relax, enjoy yourself and allow good things to enter your life.

Reflections

- Life doesn't have to be a never-ending obstacle course, unless that's the way you like it to be.
- Fire fighting may help us to feel in control, but ultimately it is a tiring and unrewarding business.
- *Do-aholism* keeps us nice and busy when we don't want to face our feelings.
- Real control is about being balanced.
- Discontent is always a sign that we are not running at our full potential.
- Change may be frightening but no-change can be a much more terrifying prospect!

11

Just How Perfect Can You Get?

'I know if I can do it just one more time, I can get it completely right.'

ANONYMOUS

Although this chapter is about women it will certainly be of interest to any man who wants to understand women!

When it's totally perfect I will be content; when I lose more weight, then I will be happy; I must look absolutely right; the house must be immaculate; I need to cook a first-class meal; everything must be totally together ... I must be Superwoman!

Do you recognize yourself here? Are you juggling career, partner, social life, family, children, plates full of food, dirty clothes and anything and everything else in a quest to become the most perfect woman you could ever wish to meet? Do you set yourself standards by which you judge the value of your days? Are you always striving to achieve more? Do you ever give yourself a break? Try this exercise.

Superwoman quiz

1. Friends are coming to dinner.

Do you have to clean the house, cook something exotic and complicated and wear yourself out?

Or do you take a more relaxed approach and expect your friends to take you as they find you and share a simple, easy to prepare meal?

2. You are feeling exhausted.

Do you carry on regardless?

Or do you give up and go to bed?

3. Do you think that you would be happier and more successful if you lost weight?

4. Do you feel incomplete if you aren't wearing make-up?

5. Do you sometimes push yourself beyond your limits?

6. Is it important to you that people think that you are always in control?

7. Do you ever feel that you are not good enough?

8. Would you describe yourself as a perfectionist?

Why women can't stop trying to be 'good enough'

So often we women struggle with a desire to please those around us in order to keep everyone happy. How many men do you know who do this? Striving for perfection will always leave you miserable, exhausted, angry, unfulfilled and never satisfied (these things you know).

The root of our problem lies in an addiction: we are addicted to *constant comparison shopping*. Before we pursue this, take a look at these questions:

- Do you ever use words like 'average' or 'normal' to describe yourself?
- Do you often wish that you looked like someone else?
- Do you try to be like other people so that you can fit in?
- Are you constantly unhappy with the size and shape of your body?
- Do you ever wear fashionable clothes even though they don't suit you?
- Do you ever feel jealous of the achievements of others?
- Are you afraid to rock the boat?

Did you have any 'yes' answers? Of course you did; we all suffer from a common affliction: comparing ourselves with others to decide how we should run our own lives. Why do we put ourselves through this comparison ordeal? Twenty-first-century woman is surrounded by glitzy lifestyle images of airbrushed perfection: how she should look, the 'right' shaped breasts/nose/legs, the most up-to-date kitchen equipment/fashionable clothes/trendy food ... This list is endless and meaningless. If we pursue the lifestyle dream of 'having it all' we will spend our whole life trying to keep up with media hype and we will always feel unhappy, unfulfilled, dissatisfied and low in confidence.

Just watch those TV adverts telling you that if you only use product X you too will look as beautiful/ be as confident/ appear as young/feel as fabulous as ... whom? Let's face it, when we are feeling a bit low it's easy to start comparing ourselves unfavourably with others. And off we go, comparison shopping: buying into the idea of a comparative scale of self-worth. It goes something like this:

'I'm not as gorgeous as ... but I'm prettier than ...'

'I'm not good enough/thin enough/clever enough to do that.'

'I'm not really intelligent but I'm cleverer than ...'

No wonder we are never satisfied; how can we be happy with ourselves and our lives if there is always somebody 'better' than us? While we live a competitive race that we must strive to win, we will never ever be 'good enough'. Perfectionists are always losers who become victimized by their impossible quest.

10 ways to give yourself a break

1. Know that you are special. Stop comparison shopping and start living by your own lights. Control your natural desire to compare yourself with others; the important thing to remember is that you are good enough just the way you are. There is no need to try to become someone else, you are unique and special, just believe this to be true.

2. Repeat the following mantra: 'I am happy to be me.' Say it, sing it, shout it, write it as many times a day as you can! Your sense of inner strength and self-belief will increase and you will begin to let go of the need to compete.

3. Enjoy the glitz and glamour of the 21st-century lifestyle but keep this in perspective. Contentment and happiness can't be bought from any store and money can't buy you love. In other words, don't let the material world distract you from your main purpose: to live a full and creative life.

4. Learn to recognize the difference between achieving important goals and ruining your life (and the life of your loved ones) by pushing yourself beyond your limits.

5. Tune in to your feelings and you will know when you have gone too far. When you are feeling stretched just stop and ask yourself, 'How important is this'? If you're not feeling good does it really matter if the floor is dirty? So you aren't looking your best, does this have to ruin your day?

6. Take a reality check. Why does your life have to stay on hold until you are the perfect weight, have the perfect qualifications, have the perfect relationship, live in the perfect house ...? Perhaps waiting to be perfect is a way out of taking your next important step. Sometimes the risk of change feels so challenging that we will come up with anything to delay it. Just check that you aren't doing this.

7. Decide to stop wasting your time. Life is shorter than we think and we need to get on with the business of living. Perfectionists set unrealistic goals and so are bound to fail: they are always disappointed – in life, in themselves and in others. If you maintain impossible standards throughout your life you will have wasted your precious gift.

8. Let go of the need to control everything. This is such a great tip! What a relief to put down all those burdens. Yes, you are not indispensable (the world will keep turning after you have gone). Feeling and looking in control can become an obsessive desire. Often we use the appearance of control in order to hide our vulnerability and hurt. You can start to let go (mentally and physically) in small ways; no need to get into a panic, just let go a bit at a time. This will become

easier and easier and so will your life!

9. Allow yourself to *be* yourself. Don't waste your life trying to be Superwoman or some other mythical creature who is more talented/more beautiful/more deserving than you! Drop those defences and accept the real you: she is fabulous, talented and truly amazing!

10. Enjoy yourself. All this competition-entering has turned us into very worried bunnies with such important concerns as: *does my bum look too big in this? Am I too fat to wear a swimming costume? Is this piece of work really good enough or do I need to go over and over it just in case? Does he think I'm boring? How can I ever look as beautiful as Catherine Zeta Jones?* Imagine giving advice to a grown-up daughter; now give that advice to yourself. Learn to be the woman you really are.

Reflections

- Do you set yourself impossible standards?
- If we pursue the lifestyle dream of 'having it all' we will spend our whole life trying to keep up with media hype.
- Perfectionists are always losers.
- Stop comparison shopping and live by your own lights.
- Why does your life have to stay on hold until you get everything perfect *once and for all?* You will have to wait forever!
- If you maintain impossible standards throughout your life, you will have wasted your precious gift.

12

Following the Path
With a Heart

*'We must make certain that our path is
connected with our heart ... When we
ask, "Am I following a path with
heart?" we discover that no one can
define for us exactly what our path
should be ...
If we are still and listen deeply, even
for a moment, we will know if we are
following a path with heart.'*

JACK KORNFIELD

We call ourselves human *beings* and not human *doings*. We are
spiritual beings learning how to live in the material world.
However, we act as if the reverse was true: we act as if we were
physical entities who need to learn how to become spiritual.

The present widespread interest in the search for spiritual
awakening leads us in many directions and encompasses
numerous techniques. What does it mean when we say that we
are looking for our spiritual path? There are so many 'spiritual

paths' on offer; how do we choose the right one for us and how do we know when we are actually 'on' this path? Perhaps it would be more helpful to think of it in a different way. When we are looking for spiritual direction we are searching for our own truth and we can find elements of this in many pursuits. We may start to study a meditative discipline such as yoga or tai chi, go for long walks, create a garden, read spiritual books, meditate regularly, start knitting, take up painting, learn the tango, take singing lessons ... Whenever we learn to sanctify and celebrate our moments we experience the divinity in our everyday life.

Open hearts, open minds

Our spiritual journey is an unfolding process that reveals itself along many winding routes. The keys to our enlightenment lie in the places where we are true to ourselves; on any path that has a heart. A client, Sarah, once told me that her heart felt closed by grief and betrayal and she didn't know how to draw on her spiritual strength any more because she felt that none of her life paths led to or from her heart. When we are feeling sad, disillusioned, let down, alone and unsupported it is very hard to connect with our spirituality, and yet it is at this time that we most need to touch our divine essence. Our connection with our Higher Self is *always there*; it's just that we lose trust and faith. I asked Sarah to draw a big heart in the middle of a page and then to create a spidergram of her heartlines (the things that moved her emotions and that she felt passionate about).

As soon as she drew her heart at the centre of the paper, her spirit seemed to lift (the shape of a heart is deeply evocative) and it didn't take long to fill in her heartlines. Opening her heart helped Sarah to open her mind, and so she began to lift out of

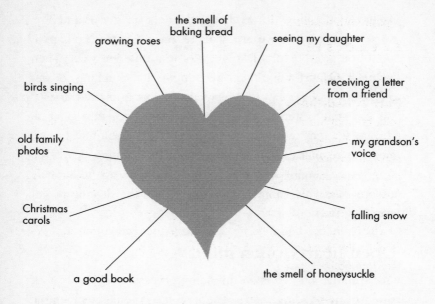

the smell of
baking bread

seeing my daughter

growing roses

receiving a letter
from a friend

birds singing

old family
photos

my grandson's
voice

Christmas
carols

falling snow

a good book

the smell of honeysuckle

depression and feel her spiritual connection once more.

Figure 4: Heartlines Spidergram

Finding your own paths with a heart

Our passions and delights keep our hearts open. Have you ever
spent time with someone who kept complaining and blaming?
How did you feel after your encounter? And now think of a
person you know who is full of life and positivity. Isn't she just
a joy to be around? Whenever we are fascinated and enthusiastic about anything in our life we become fascinating to others.
Our enthusiasm is catching. When we are tuned into the energy
of our heart there is a change in our magnetic field so that we
both attract and resonate with the good in ourselves and in
others. This means that we 'know' how to act at each moment;
we can reach for the highest in others and in ourselves; we
instinctively make the right decisions and so we naturally follow

a path with a heart.

Heart opener

Part 1: heartlines spidergram

Look back at Sarah's heartlines spidergram. Consider some of the
things that moved her heart: the smell of baking bread, falling
snow, the voice of her grandson ... Seemingly ordinary
experiences can really touch our soul, can't they? What touches
your soul? Don't think about this too much, just draw your own
heartlines spidergram and see what emerges on the paper.
Ordinary life can be so extraordinary, we just need to look in a
slightly different way. Opening your heart will always set you on
the right path.

Part 2: world heart embrace

Stand up and really stretch. Now, inhale deeply and hold out your
arms as wide as you can. Imagine that you are embracing the
whole world. Hold the stretch and this vision as long as you can
hold your breath. As you exhale, bring your arms slowly, gently
and lovingly together so that your hands fold over each other on
your chest. You have brought the love of the whole world into your
own heart; feel it enter every part of your body. Spend a few
moments appreciating the feeling of warmth and wellbeing.

Repeat these actions again. As you inhale and stretch know
that you are sending out love to the universe, and as you exhale
and bring your hands to your chest that you are receiving the love
of the world.

This is a beautiful exercise, do it whenever time and location
permit. Love flows through us continually, allow yourself to become
aware of it and your connection with the universal life force will
amaze you.

Doe Lang says of this exercise: 'This is the most life-affirming
gesture, the primal loving welcome of the eternal mother. Muscle
testing shows that merely seeing this gesture strengthens your life

force.'

Is this a path with a heart?

We do not always feel brimming with the love of the universe. Life throws many challenges our way and on such a day we still have to make important decisions and choices. Sometimes we act out of fear instead of love: perhaps we behave badly towards someone to cause them pain, find ourselves unable to express our true feelings or just float off course so that we don't fulfil our commitments. So it is easy to find that we have left our heart path and are drifting into negativity, depression, boredom and low self-esteem. As soon as you begin to feel less than your best, recognize your symptoms and then check the true nature of your present path. On a path with a heart:

- You feel good.
- Relationships are supportive.
- You feel positive and enthusiastic (even if things don't always go perfectly).
- There is an overall awareness that you are 'going with the flow'.

Take any challenging area of your life (we all have these) and check for the above points. If, for example, you are very unhappy at work and, although your workmates are supportive, you just can't seem to feel enthusiastic about your job, then obviously something is wrong. Your heart is not in this particular career choice. So why do you stay in this job? Boredom? Inertia? Fear of change? You need to question your behaviour and decide to be true to yourself.

Apply this procedure to any part of your life that feels

unhappy – and remember: if your heart is not in it, your life will never feel worth living.

Ask yourself some searching questions. Challenge your own behaviour and actions: why are you being untrue to yourself? Seek some answers; be true to yourself. Take courage. Take the path with a heart.

Reflections

- When you are seeking spiritual direction you are searching for your own truth.
- Our enlightenment lies in the places where we are true to ourselves; on any path that has a heart.
- When we are tuned into our heart energy our magnetic field changes so that we attract and resonate with all that is good.
- If you want to feel fabulous, just do something you are longing to do.
- Your ordinary life can feel quite extraordinary – your ordinary life *is* quite extraordinary.
- If your heart is not in it, your life will never feel worth living.

13

Too Busy to Be Happy

' *"Well in our country," said Alice, still panting a little, "you'd generally get to somewhere else – if you ran very fast for a long time, as we've been doing."*

' *"A slow sort of country!" said the Queen. "Now, here, you see, it takes all the running you can do to keep in the same place. If you want to get somewhere else, you must run at least twice as fast as that!" '*

LEWIS CARROLL

As we run from pillar to post and back again, we can only be grateful that we don't live in Lewis Carroll's Looking Glass World. But it often feels as if we do: the notion of running at top speed in order to stay in the same place feels strangely familiar. Do you recognize this feeling of having to keep up with a certain pace of activity *just to keep things as they are?* How can we ever find the motivation and energy to set and achieve new goals? When we are busy running to keep up with our career, finances, relationships, exercise, family, how can we make time for ... well, for our life?

Are you afraid to stop?

If you stopped trying to be the best juggler in town, what do you think might happen? Would the sky fall in if you didn't get everything on the shopping list, make a quick snack for dinner, clear your in-tray by going home time, clean the floor, pick up your dry cleaning, do the washing? ... If you couldn't bothered to do anything because you were too wiped out and spent the afternoon in bed?

Ah, but there's so much to do! Yes, I agree, but surely it's time to take a stand when our lives become nothing more than a succession of repeated chores: there will *always* be more to do while we draw breath.

I know when I have reached the heights of my 'doing' madness. The penny drops on those days when I find myself doing any combination of the following: trying to clean my teeth *at the same time as* filling the washing machine; having a telephone conversation *at the same time* as writing an email; interrupting one activity when I glimpse something else that really *can't wait a moment longer*. Such a day has a buzzy, frazzled feel to it and after a short while there are piles of projects lying around in an unfinished state. One other unmistakeable sign is my total exhaustion (after the initial energetic burst). Oh yes, it's time stop!

Drifting off

On a day when you are over 'doing' it, you will recognize your own symptoms; stop before they turn into a headache or anything equally unpleasant. Let the signs be a warning to you and take immediate action (or rather, inaction). Take a few moments to stand and stare (the world won't stop just because you have). Yes, you can easily find the time. When you incorporate 'being' time into your 'doing' time you will find that everything flows much more smoothly. Remember that we are operating at three interdependent levels: mind, body and spirit. Excessive thinking and doing leaves us out of balance in the spiritual department. Daydreaming and drifting time are food for the spirit, so include some free-floating moments in your busy day. Try it now. Soften your gaze, let go of your thoughts and allow yourself to drift off for a few seconds. It doesn't take long to create a more balanced awareness, which will then help you to put everything back into perspective. Begin to incorporate 'standing and staring' time into your everyday activities and you will feel more relaxed and in control.

Seven reasons why you might be afraid to stop

1. Desire to 'get it right, once and for all'. This is another slant on the perfectionist theme. If you are a person who is never *quite* satisfied with what you do, you may be locked into a cycle of 'must try harder'. This will keep you 100 per cent busy in a quest to finally achieve 10 out of 10. Workaholics will recognize this syndrome. Is your best ever good enough for you? If not, it's time to let yourself off the hook.

2. Unrealistic self-expectations. It's good to have positive expectations but modern society has created a new pressure: the phenomenon of unrealistic expectations. For example, when the media promises the possibility of becoming a millionaire by answering a few simple

questions, winning a recording contract even if you can't sing, or becoming famous overnight for doing absolutely nothing, we can easily become dissatisfied with our lot. Are you wearing yourself out making comparisons with others and overachieving to try to gain an unrealistic 'success' that you think you deserve?

3. Fear of change. Although the *idea* of change can often feel exhilarating, the prospect of coping with the unknown can often cause anxiety. When we are afraid of change we can find any number of cunning plans to delay taking action: we have to do this and that and the other; we have to keep busy because there is always more to do *and no time to do anything different*. Is your fear of change creating your busyness?

4. Too anxious to delegate. Yes, you're right, no one can do the job in the same way that you can. But this doesn't mean that you can't delegate. So the children may need nagging while they learn how to do some household chores and they will never make their beds as well as you do, but they will soon find out what it's like to sleep in a crumpled bed, and it's one job less for you! If you are overloaded at work, then who on your team can help you? And if there is no one available to share your load, stop and consider whether you are being asked to do too much. Do you need to make some changes?

   You are not indispensable; no one is! Let this thought help you to share your burdens.

5. Fear of intimacy. Excessive busyness keeps relation-ships at bay: there's no time to get close because there's just too much to do. Sometimes when we are faced with an emotional problem we find relief in 'losing ourselves' in doing something, and this often helps us to sort things out. But if we keep filling up

our time by escaping into a whirlwind of activity, we create an impenetrable boundary through which others are unable to reach us. Don't be afraid to get in touch with your feelings. Face your own emotions, be yourself and you will feel so much better.

6. Needing to be needed. It may be hard to recognize this condition, which is sometimes called the Rescuer Syndrome. Whenever we help and encourage another person we are showing our humanity in the very finest way. Metaphorically speaking, we are giving people fishing lines rather than fish, in order that they can become independent. Caring is always about helping people to stand on their own feet and to make their own mistakes if they have to. Occasionally the boundary lines become blurred: another person needs more than we can or should give; we feel guilty that we can never do enough for them; we need them to need us because it gives meaning to our life; we get lost in worrying about their problems so that we don't have to look at our own. Check your personal boundaries. Let go when it is appropriate. And keep in mind, that every time you try to rescue someone you are treating them as if they are a victim. Rescuing can become a full time activity; make sure this doesn't happen to you.

7. Believing that life can't be fun. If you are a glass-half-empty rather than a glass-half-full sort of person, you will find it very easy to see all the things that have yet to be done (there will always be things that need doing). Do-aholics believe that they can only have fun *after* the work is done, and that seems to be never. Life can be as fun as you make it! Try this: rather than being fixated on what has to be done, why not focus on what has already been achieved. Appreciate and savour your achievements: let your glass be half full!

EXERCISE:

Be here now

Being too busy to be happy has become a very bad habit for
many of us. But this exercise can help to break this behaviour
pattern.

When the doing gets too much and your life is running out of
control, stop and say to yourself, 'Be here now!' This little phrase
will place you at the very centre of the present moment. Recognize
this perfect moment of your life right now. Feel the now. There
really is nothing else: the past is gone and the future doesn't exist
(it will always lie around the corner). Repeating this mantra will
help you to stay consciously in the present – the only place where
you can truly appreciate your precious life.

Slow down, take it easy and know that your life can be fun.

Reflections

- Make time for your life.
- The sky won't fall in if you stop being busy.
- Daydreaming and drifting time are food for the spirit,
  so include some free-floating moments in your busy
  day.
- You are not indispensable; let this thought help you to
  let go.
- Every time you rescue someone you are treating them
  like a victim.
- Be here now!

14

Men Are From Mars (Communication Skills for Venusians)

'One of the biggest challenges for men is correctly to interpret and support a woman when she is talking about her feelings. The biggest challenge for women is correctly to interpret and support a man when he isn't talking.'

JOHN GRAY

What single thing would most improve the quality of your life? A recent survey by a women's magazine reveals that 60 per cent of women answering this question asked only *that their partner would spend just 15 minutes a day talking to them 'meaningfully'*. While this might not be exactly top of your wish list if you were ever to encounter the genie of the lamp (I'm thinking more along the lines of bags of confidence, charisma, status, stunning looks, fulfilling career, happiness, health, wealth, etc.), it does highlight what seems to be an almost universal problem for women: how can we encourage our men to talk to us about their feelings?

Men and women are different

On average, men speak 12,000 words a day, while women speak 23,000 words. I'm sure that the difference in these statistics is of no surprise to you, and some of us may even consider 12,000 to be a rather optimistic figure! Further research has shown that while women automatically direct their emotions to that part of the brain that lets them talk about their feelings (as they are experiencing them), *men can't do this*. So, instead of talking about his feelings your man will channel his emotions into actions (you didn't need me to tell you this). Remember the last time you were really getting into a good row and he suddenly upped and left (to see his mates, go for a drive, have a drink, just *do* something)? And then he comes back and he's forgotten all about the row and you're still seething. How utterly frustrating this can be. Well, what's to be done? Given the physiological differences of our brains, *can* anything be done?

EXERCISE:

Getting men to talk

Yes, you can get your man to talk, but you must plan your approach discreetly.

- Don't make statements like 'You never tell me how you feel' or 'Why don't we talk more' or even 'Why don't we plan some time to talk?' These may be interpreted as criticism and will close down the lines of communication immediately.

- Organize talk time. Create some time in your busy schedules where you can be intimate and attentive to one another. Be subtle, recreate your early dating days and give him your full attention (men love this). Ask him about his activities – this can lead to greater things. Don't expect too much at once.

- And once he starts chatting, let him talk! Resist all temptation to empathize with him. Women fall automatically into 'overlapping' mode when they talk to each other. Your friend discloses a problem and you say something like 'I know exactly what you are going through.' We do this with each other to show support and it brings us closer together. Beware, men hate this technique. Resist the temptation to jump in there or he will close up and it will be you who is doing all the talking (again). Learn to listen well and leave some spaces for him to talk into.

- Remember that men and women communicate differently. Men speak to give information and women speak to create emotional bonds. Keep this in mind.

What women want

In the film *What Women Want*, Mel Gibson plays an ad man who can read the minds of the women around him and so can at last find out what women want. Three things spring to my mind immediately. First, men don't have to wait until they develop telepathic powers to know what women want – they can just ask! Second, would we want men to know exactly what we are thinking? I like my partner to know when I want cuddles, attention, long intimate chats, perfume, help in the kitchen, home improvements ... but there are lots of things I don't want him to know (plans to spend a lot of money on that gorgeously frivolous pair of shoes, secret fantasies about Johnny Depp and chocolate, passing concerns over increasing wrinkles and droopy bits ...). Third, all that matters is that *we* know what we want. And this is the most important point. We are certainly better off without telepathic men because then we can choose which of our thoughts to share.

When you are not getting what you want

If your intimate relationship is not all that you would wish it to be (the man in your life just isn't coming up with the goods), something has to give, and that doesn't have to be you. If you are fed up with living with an ostrich (with his head in the sand or the newspaper) it's time to come clean with your want list. You can't get what you want unless you can communicate your needs clearly, and this may mean taking a new assertive and tactful approach.

Write a list of all the things you want from your relationship. For example: *I want more emotional support, I want you to help around the house, I want to go out with you once a week* ...You may be surprised by what you come up with. Women are not trained to put their needs first (we are always so busy looking after someone else). This time, put yourself first and stand up for what you want, but do it diplomatically. Don't read out your list in anger (this will never bring the changes you want). Take one item at a time and communicate each of your needs in a way that is effective. Rather than criticizing ('you never take me out anywhere'), use a supportive approach ('I love going out with you; where shall we go this week?'). Know what you want and communicate your needs in a creative way and you are more likely get what you want.

Vive la différence!

Women speak the same language and it's usually emotionally driven. We are experts at using both sides of our brain at once and so we can articulate our emotions as we feel them. Out with a girlfriend, chatting to my mother or my grown-up daughter, in casual conversation with a woman at the gym, I know where the discussion is going – *women speak the same language* And men speak another language. Never forget that men and women are different and always remember that men are unable to use both sides of their brain at the same time! This physiological fact has an important effect on women's relationships with men because it means that men can be logical *or* emotional but they can't make spontaneous connections with their feelings and their rationality and so they cannot express their emotions as they are feeling them. My single tip is to *stop expecting the impossible*: men will never be like women (and who would want them to be?) Use your knowledge of our gender differences to smooth and harmonize your relationships with men and enjoy our diverse experiences. Appreciate male power and flaunt and celebrate your female power, and may the relationship between the sexes stay ever vibrant, challenging and exciting! *Vive la différence!*

Reflections

- Men speak to give information and women speak to create emotional bonds.
- Men cannot express their emotions as they are feeling them (confusing for women).
- But women can and do express their emotions as they are feeling them (confusing for men).
- Learn to listen well and leave some spaces for him to talk into.
- Never criticize, as this will always lead to communication breakdown.
- Stop expecting the impossible: men will never be like women. And for this we should be grateful.

15

Seeing the Light at the End of the Tunnel

Hope is the thing with feathers—

That perches in the soul—

And sings the tune without the words—

And never stops at all—

EMILY DICKINSON

On the beautiful Greek island of Rhodes is a lush beauty spot nestling in pine woods. Epta Piges (Seven Springs) is a luxuriant green haven, a wonderful pace to go when the sun is just too hot to handle. The water at the source of each spring is so clear and delicious that tourists get busy emptying their (bought) bottles of water and refilling them. The seven springs become a stream that flows through a beautiful arched tunnel about a metre wide and two metres high. In her *Insight Pocket Guide of Rhodes*, Susanne Heidelck, speaking about the light green pool that lies at the end of the stream says, 'Those not afraid to roll up their trousers and wade into the dark will be rewarded by what they find on the other side of the tunnel. However, the faint at heart can reach the pool more easily by simply climbing the hill.'

Of course I was intrigued and enraptured by these two sentences, and so Epta Piges became a 'must do' tourist attraction for my family and I. Determined to demonstrate strength of character, we rolled up our trousers and, carrying our sandals, waded forth into the cold water. The tunnel is narrow and cold and has a few bends, so very soon we were in complete darkness. And so we shuffled along looking for the light that we knew would be there at the end of the tunnel. How amazing to step out of that narrow, wet, dark place into a bright green pool shimmering in the sunlight ... Mmmm! Definitely well worth the 200-metre paddle in the dark. And waiting to greet us and ask us what it was like in the tunnel was an international crowd of folk who had got there by 'simply climbing the hill'.

Life can be hard. We can face setbacks, calamities and tragedies and still be expected to appear for breakfast, go to work, do the washing, keep a brave face. We don't always have the choice to go by tunnel or take the easy route. When our lives are getting us down and there just doesn't seem to be anything to lift our spirits (we can't see the light at the end of the tunnel) we only have the depth of our faith, hope and trust to turn to. If we are strong in self-belief and hold a positive world-view, then we have an anchor and can weather any storm. However badly we feel, we will know and understand at a very deep level that *this too will pass*.

Writer Julia Cameron calls positive thinking a form of spiritual muscle and I think this is a very useful image to hold. When depression strikes it feeds all our negative patterns and takes us into the darkness of the negative cycle where faith, hope and trust can't be seen. This really is what depression is all about: the dark night of the soul when we can't hear 'the thing with feathers' even though it never stops singing. Negativity weakens our spiritual muscles and positivity develops them. Consider positive thinking exercises as a form of spiritual workout. It may feel painful at the start and you may want to give up, but reflect upon the wonderful benefits. Strong spiritual muscles increase your deposits of faith, hope and trust, and when the next challenge knocks at your door you can call on those resources.

EXERCISE:
_____

Developing your spiritual muscles

Our self-belief and our view of the world depend largely on what we learned to believe as a child. If you were given love and support and were validated when you were tiny, you are more likely to have a good strong self-image than is someone who was criticized and invalidated. Similarly, you were 'taught' your beliefs about the world (it's a benevolent universe/life's a drag/people are basically good/everyone's out to get you ...). What sort of pictures of the world were you brought up with?

Change any negative self-images; they will always stand in the way of your spiritual development. The way to do this is very simple. Just pinpoint your negative self-beliefs, throw them out and replace them with positive self-beliefs. What could be easier? Don't get wrapped up in an intellectual or emotional game with yourself. Negative beliefs serve no purpose. You were taught to believe they were true and now you believe them. That's all there is to it. Teach yourself something more useful.

List all the self-beliefs that don't work for you. For example:

MY NEGATIVE SELF-BELIEFS
I'm no good at ...
I'm useless.
I can't do that.
Trust me to make a mess of it.

These sorts of beliefs will make it impossible to develop the spiritual muscles necessary to cope with the dark patches we will inevitably encounter at some time in our life. How can we believe that we have strong inner resources (which of course we have) if we think that we are useless, stupid, untrustworthy, no good, etc.? Replace your negative affirmations with positive ones. Write your replacements in a second column so that your list looks like this:

MY NEGATIVE SELF-BELIEFS	REPLACEMENTS
I'm no good at …	I'm getting better at …
I'm useless.	I'm a creative person.
I can't do that.	I'll do the best I can.
Trust me to make a mess of it.	I can make a good job of this.

Now cross out your old list. Whenever negativity strikes, strike back with your new positive affirmations. For example, you feel afraid to tackle something and feelings of uselessness and inability creep over you. Check out your negative thoughts and stop them; start saying to yourself, 'I can do this.' So you think it won't work because you don't believe that you really can do it? That's the whole point. We are only dealing in thoughts here and always remember that thoughts can be changed. Why run with thoughts that keep you down? Read out your replacement list whenever you can. Write down your positive affirmations and say them, read them, sing them and shout them at every possible opportunity. And eventually a headful of negativity will become a headful of positivity. When the next life problem arises you will find new spiritual muscle power that you didn't have before. Yes, I can deal with this/I may feel terrible now but I will get over this/I am strong/There's a light at the end of this tunnel.

However bleak your situation, you will know and believe the amazing truth that this too will pass. And it will!

Take that leap of faith

Sometimes we are presented with a choice: take the well-trodden route, do the same thing as usual and stick to what we know, or take a risk, be courageous, change and *make some waves!* We have all faced this dilemma.

Change always feels risky as we move into uncharted territory, but staying in your comfort zone is a far greater risk. What would you like to change in your life? Job, partner, hair colour, confidence levels, fitness? Make a list. Now take each thing and ask yourself why you are stuck. Why haven't you left that boring job? Stood up to that person who is always bringing you down? Become a sultry brunette? Take your courage in both hands, decide what you want to change and then JUST DO IT! It's so easy. Some people may be put out and the going may be tough for a while. You may not be able to see the light at the end of the tunnel, but you will know it's there because courageous acts strengthen the soul.

Reflections

- Positive-thinking exercises are a form of spiritual workout.
- Strong spiritual muscles increase your deposits of faith, hope and trust.
- Negative beliefs will never work for you; throw them out and believe the best about yourself and the world.
- You are creative and courageous.
- Thoughts can always be changed.
- Your expectations will always come true, so expect the best.

16

You Are Good Enough Just the Way You Are

*'Become as resourceful in inspiring
yourself to enter your own peace
as you are at being neurotic and
competitive in the world.'*

SOGYAL RINPOCHE

My school days were strict and very disciplined. This was a time, 'back in the old days', when hands were slapped and bottoms were caned and the teacher was an all-powerful figure. We had weekly tests and sat in descending rows, our seat representing the position we had achieved that week: a constant and visible display of our glory or our shame. I was an academic child and intensely competitive and the old-fashioned ways suited me well: I so wanted praise, to be the best, to be chosen and to show that I was good enough for ...? Well, for anything and everything.

Good, better, best!

When I was ten we had a form teacher with a voice like a foghorn, a fiery temper and a fierce desire for us all to reach our potential. Mr Moore was a motivational guru, well before his time. As he swept into the classroom each morning he banged on his desk and we would all repeat the mantra he had taught us: 'Good, better, best, never let us rest, until our good is better and our better best.'

Some days I would be fired with enthusiasm by these words, but at other times I was frightened and felt inadequate to meet the challenge. There's a fine line between the wonderful expansiveness that comes as we reach for our potential, and the unbearable limitation of never ever feeling quite good enough. How do we get into that no-win situation where our best is never enough for us, where the only way to feel in control is to be perfect, even when we know that perfectionism is unattainable?

A desire to do well can become an addiction of sorts. If our ambition leads into a perpetual need to be perfect, when is our 'good' enough in itself? And when we change our 'good' into 'better' can we stop and congratulate ourselves for our success or must we ever drive ourselves onwards towards our 'best'? As my elderly aunt was fond of saying, 'Where will it all end?' Of course it ends in tears, and frustration and low self-esteem. Once we start to confuse *what we do* with *who we are* we are slipping into neurotic behaviour.

Be at peace with yourself

If you recognize a tendency to harass and harangue yourself just relax here and take a breather; you are in the majority. And if you are a woman you will almost certainly identify with the 'not good enough' syndrome. We hang ourselves from so many hooks: we are too fat, too lazy and not clever, beautiful or talented enough; we don't ever do enough and what we do is never good enough. Enough of all this! I want to tell you that *you are good enough just the way you are!* It's true, it's just that you don't believe it yet.

Everything is a question of belief; you are what you think you are. When you see someone who knows their own worth you are not looking at a natural optimist. Believe me, this is a person who has had to learn to let go of their negative self-beliefs in order to embrace positivity and self-esteem. And if they can do it so can you!

You speak with many voices

Sad, happy, loving, angry, thoughtful, responsive, critical, supportive, blaming, whining, carefree, pessimistic, enthusiastic, pacifying ... the ways we can speak to others are as diverse as our thoughts and emotions.

It is obvious to us that the way we communicate with someone affects our relationship with him or her: if we are encouraging and friendly we are much more likely to have a healthy, positive relationship than if we are critical and hurtful. But what communication skills do we use when we are relating to ourselves? Yes, we are always talking to and at ourselves in a ceaseless babble of thoughts and words: our minds do so love to chatter on! To prove the point, just close your eyes and listen to what happens. It's noisy inside your head, isn't it? The mind is very good at its job, which is to keep on thinking, observing and making inner conversation. We spend most of our lives listening to these powerful inner voices and they control and direct the way we live.

An important question to ask is 'How do I speak to myself?' If you find it hard to believe that you are constantly talking to yourself, try this. Over the next few days pay attention to your mental processes: what sort of thoughts do you have? Observe the way you think and how that goes on to affect the way you act. Are you kind to yourself? Do you forgive your mistakes and encourage yourself to move onwards or are you often looking back into the past and regretting your actions? What sort of thoughts keep you awake at night? Do you find yourself moving along fearful mental paths, worrying and expecting the worst, or is there an inner optimistic voice that brings you hope at times of uncertainty? I expect that, like all of us, you will become aware of all these voices and more. The ways in which we speak to ourselves are as many and varied as the ways in which we speak to others. And the same communication rules apply: validation creates a positive response and invalidation and criticism creates an impasse.

Recognizing your inner critic

The voice of your inner critic will be well developed and loud! We all have this voice and it is so well known that psychologists have given it a name. It speaks like this: '*You're no good; whatever makes you think you can do/be that?; it's all your fault; I hate you, you are so fat/stupid/lazy/thoughtless ...; you are unlovable; you can't trust yourself; you don't deserve anything; you will never ever be perfect ...*' etc. And when you are feeling intimidated in a social situation it is this voice that says, 'For goodness sake why don't you speak up and make your presence felt.' So you start talking, and only moments later your inner critic is telling you off again: 'Oh be quiet, won't you! Just listen to yourself rambling on; you sound such a fool.' So you stop talking and feel like an idiot. Listening to your inner critic can certainly make you feel as if you're going crazy. But you're not!

This voice speaks from your own collection of choice past criticisms that you have heard and come to believe. You may even recognize its tone as a replica of the way you were criticized as a child.

But now you are a grown-up and you can change any self-beliefs that aren't working for you. Your real and true self is balanced and centred and it knows that you are amazing. It knows that you can only reach your potential when your mind is clear and positive. Your real self speaks with a true voice and it will always support you. Even if you blow it in some way, it will remind you that you are bigger than your mistakes, and its non-critical approach ensures that you will be able adopt a creative way to change the situation. Figure 5 gives some examples of the ways in which your inner critic and your real self might talk to you.

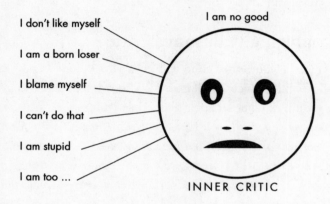

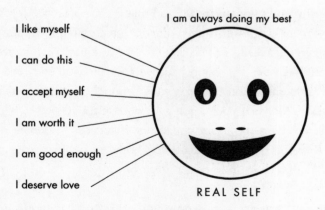

Figure 5: Inner Voices Diagram

How are you talking to yourself ?

Draw your own version of Figure 5. Fill in the messages from your own inner critic. Remember this important point: you will never please this voice; its job is to criticize you *whatever you do*, and if you listen to it you will always be a victim. Listen instead to your real self: a voice that transcends all the others. Fill in the affirmations that your real self might be giving you, even if you can't hear them at the moment. Use the messages that are given in Figure 5 if can't think of your own positive statements. Start saying these positive affirmations to yourself (act as if you believe them even if you don't yet) and slowly but surely you will let go of all those damaging, self-critical beliefs. Stop beating yourself up, be at peace with yourself, become your best and most wonderful self and know that you are *always* good enough, just the way you are!

Reflections

- When our best is never good enough we are in a no-win situation.
- If we start confusing *what we do* with *who we are*, we are slipping into neurotic behaviour.
- Everything is a question of belief; you are what you think you are.
- Your inner critic will keep on telling you off – this is its job.
- Your real and true self is balanced and centred and it knows that you are amazing.
- You deserve love.

17

Are You Addicted?

*'Addictive behaviour is another way of
saying, "I'm not good enough." '*

With her usual clarity, Louise Hay goes straight to the heart of
the matter, no fancy jargon, no beating about the bush: yes,
addictive behaviour is a complex issue but when we get right
down to its roots we always find self-hate and low self-esteem.

We can be addicted to so many things: eating or not eating, abusive love relationships, drink, sex, drugs (prescribed or illegal),
over-working, over-exercising, over-spending, over-nurturing,
busyness ... there are endless possibilities. But at the source of
any addiction we will always discover the victim pattern.

About addictions

- Most addictions are perceived by the addicted person
  as life-enhancing but are really soul-destroying.
- Addictive behaviour is rooted in self-hate, and an
  addicted person has low self-esteem.
- If we give away our personal power we will always be
  trying to fill that empty space.
- We become addicted to compensate for the lack of
  fulfilment of our emotional needs.
- If we are compulsively using any behaviour to hide

from our true feelings and to punish ourselves then we are addicted.

- Some addictions are life-threatening and others threaten the quality of our life.

The dysfunctional family

Whatever we learn to believe about ourselves and the universe we learn in our early years. If you come from a family that was nurturing and supportive, you are much more likely to be able to trust yourself and others. This positive pattern encourages feelings of self-esteem and self-belief, which create a healthy attitude to life.

An addict is ruled by negative thoughts, beliefs and emotional patterns that she developed in early childhood. The term 'dysfunctional' is often used to describe a family that is non-supportive, inflexible and runs on fear. Such a family exhibits certain specific characteristics:

- Needs are not recognized or met.
- Behaviour is critical and invalidating.
- Feelings are not expressed.
- Low self-esteem prevails.

The child who comes from a dysfunctional family learns that she cannot trust her own instincts and perceptions and that the world is a scary place. We cannot be surprised if such a child grows up looking for a way to anaesthetize her pain.

Those with an addiction are demonstrating a deep self-hatred. How is it possible to love and respect yourself if you have been taught that you will never be 'good enough'? Low self-esteem leads into a negative spiral so that those who have an addiction problem are permanently insecure and fearful of life. How is it possible to trust others if we have never experienced those deep feelings of security and trust as a child? Whatever we believe and expect to be true will come true for us in some way, and those early wounds create a feeling of emptiness which the addict is always trying (unsuccessfully) to fill.

There are numerous support programmes available for those who recognize that they need help. Here we can only hope to open up the subject and consider some of the negative patterning that is inevitably involved.

EXERCISE:

My addictions

You may have a chocolate habit or an abusive relationship habit; addictions come in many shapes and forms. While we cannot compare our addictive behaviour, we need to accept the fact that if we are acting compulsively in any way in order to punish ourselves and numb our pain, we are addicted. If you think that this description applies to you, answer the following questions. Don't feel ashamed, many of us have a victim streak that leads us into addictive patterns (it's very common to have several addictions running along together).

1. My addictions are: . . . .

2. Do you keep your addictions secret?   Yes/No

3. If your addictions are secret, why are they?

. . . .

4. How do you feel about yourself and your addictions?

. . . .

5. Is it possible to imagine your life without your addictions?   Yes/No

6. Have you ever tried to break your addictions?   Yes/No

7. Would you like to break your addictive patterning?
Yes/No

If we have addictive patterns it is because we are in emotional pain. The addiction numbs the pain (momentarily) and this is why we are so afraid to let go of our chosen anaesthetic. Whether you need medical help or professional support of another kind, know that the help is there when you are ready. You will be amazed to know just how many other people are also acting out your 'secret' behaviours.

Loving yourself

When we can love ourselves just the way we are, we can move mountains (and give up our addictions). Our secrets and our shame reinforce our self-hatred as we go down that negative addictive spiral. Figure 6 shows how this works.

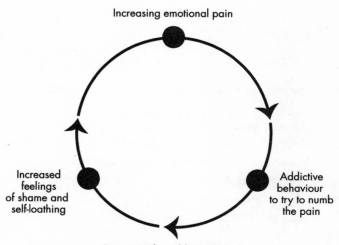

Figure 6: The Addictive Spiral

The addictive spiral

The key to breaking the addictive spiral lies in your ability to love yourself *just as you are right now* and to find self-forgiveness in your heart. However terrible your shameful secrets, just remember that your true self is still shining through. Beyond the pain and self-recriminations lies a fabulous and loving person who wants to live her best life. Why don't you let her? She has been struggling but she can give up the struggle now. Let love into your own heart and let go of your victim patterns; when you are victimizing yourself you are your own worst enemy. Start to become your own best friend. If it sounds impossible just try this:

Imagine yourself enacting your most terrible secret behaviour. Watch yourself acting out your pain and say the following affirmation: 'I love and forgive you.' Repeat this affirmation as many times as you can remember, every single day. And consider this: no person and no thing has any power over you unless you give them that power.

EXERCISE:

An action plan for change

Use this five-step plan to help you to evaluate your situation.

Step 1: assess your circumstances
Describe your relationship with your addiction.

Step 2: decide what you want to change
What don't you like about your condition? Be sure to ignore all unhelpful thoughts (such as how hard or even impossible it is to change).

Step 3: state your preferred outcome

How do you want things to change? Be assertive, positive and be as specific as possible (yes, you really can change).

Step 4: recognize the negative patterning involved

When you can do this you are on the road to recovery (and you are brave to have got this far). Self-loathing and disgust, lack of trust, the need to fill the empty space inside, the desire to be in control (ironic though this might seem), intense fear and a need to punish yourself are some of the things that brought you here.

Step 5: decide to re-pattern your life

Each one of us is working to change our negative patterns as we develop and evolve. If you look at it this way, then we are all addicts (we are addicted to repeating patterns). But whether your addiction threatens your life or ruins it in another way, only you will know if you need professional assistance to change your patterns. Go and seek help if you need it, and remember that you are not alone. You can do this!

Reflections

- Addictive behaviour is rooted in self-hate.
- If we give away our personal power we will always be trying to fill that empty space.
- Low self-esteem leads into a negative spiral so that those who have an addiction problem are permanently insecure and fearful of life.
- The wounds of early childhood create a feeling of emptiness which the addict is always trying (unsuccessfully) to fill.
- However terrible your shameful secrets, always remember that your true self is shining through.
- No person and no thing has any power over you unless you give them that power.

18

Creating Good Vibrations

'No pessimist ever discovered the secrets of the stars, or sailed to an uncharted land, or opened a new heaven to the human spirit.'

HELEN KELLER

Is your cup half full or half empty? Is your cake half eaten or have you still got half left? In other words, would you say that you are an optimist or a pessimist? Most of us are a bit of both. We can wake up feeling good, sing in the shower, smile at the world ... and the world will smile back; on such a day we can cope with whatever life throws at us. When things are not so good it's harder to keep upbeat and easy to fall into a cycle of depression.

Making good and bad vibrations

Now let's take an ordinary day when nothing is particularly terrible or wonderful. You wake up and ... how do you greet the day? Is this a perfect day or just 24 hours of hassle? Is your life a precious gift or are you just struggling to survive? Believe it or not, you can *choose* the quality of your experiences: it's not *what* happens to you that counts but rather how you deal with what happens to you. Figure 7 demonstrates how the Law of Attraction works.

This Law states that *we create whatever we think about.* We live within an electromagnetic field and each thought we have charges the energy field with vibrations. Like attracts like – this is the reason why grumpy people really *are* always having such

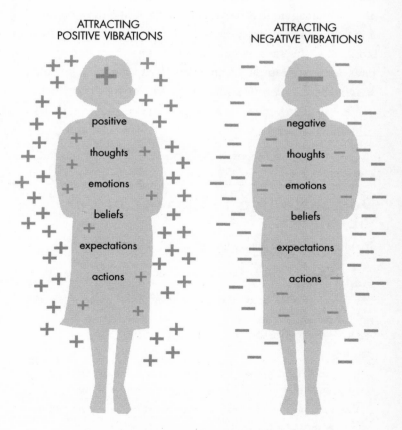

Figure 7: Attracting Good and Bad Vibrations

a bad time (negative thought patterns attract all forms of negativity) and why upbeat people attract good vibrations (positive thought patterns attract all forms of positivity). So positive thinking is more than just a fancy self-help term; it is a powerful tool that will attract the very best into your life.

In *The Charisma Book,* Doe Lang uses an interesting analogy to explain the way that negative thinking disempowers and diminishes us. She asks us to imagine a garden hose spraying water full force. The force of the spray is very powerful and the water shoots across the garden in a magnificently concentrated arc. Now imagine that you make a kink in the hose by bending it at some point along its line; the water will then slow down or stop. This, she says, is equivalent to what happens when you have a negative thought and your body tenses. *Your electromagnetic field literally weakens.* As well as this, your breathing becomes shallower and less oxygen reaches your brain, so you can't think clearly.

EXERCISE:

Demonstrating the power of our vibrations

Try this experiment with a friend.

Step 1
Stand facing each other and put your left hand on your friend's right shoulder.

Step 2
Ask her to extend her left hand, palm down, elbow straight and wrist slightly higher than her shoulder. (It doesn't matter which side of the body you use as long as your hand rests on your partner's opposite shoulder.)

Step 3

Now ask her to think of something that makes her feel really good (she should close her eyes and imagine this as clearly as possible). When she's ready, tell her that you are going to try to push down her extended hand and that she should resist this pressure (her eyes can be opened or closed).

Step 4

Place your fingers on her arm just beyond her wrist (between wrist and elbow) and press down. Make a note of the power of her resistance.

Step 5

Now ask your friend to close her eyes and think of something very negative. When she's ready repeat the process, putting your right hand on her arm and pressing down. You will both be amazed when her arm goes straight down with no strength in it at all. Reverse roles and watch it happen again!

This incredibly simple experiment demonstrates how profoundly we are affected by positive and negative thoughts and feelings.

How to create good vibrations

Norman Vincent Peale, the guru of positive thinking, makes the following fascinating observation: 'Well, it is a fact that if you love life, life will indeed love you back. You will get a terrific lift in the spirit, so much so that you will have perpetual excitement and a deep feeling of happiness. With acute sensitivity you will be able to maintain a constant and eager delight in the world and in people. This lift of the spirit will condition you to upper-level experience.'

Mmmm ... this 'upper-level experience' sounds like just the

thing that we are all after. As the quality of our experience does not depend on *what* happens to us but rather on how we process, understand and deal with what happens to us, we can choose to create a positive or a negative reality just by our attitude. Love, appreciation, enthusiasm and zest for life do indeed generate 'a terrific lift in the spirit', so let's see how we can put all this good theoretical advice into practice.

All things bright and beautiful

Just for today decide to appreciate all the good things in your life.

- Open your eyes and be glad to be alive.
- Step into the shower and enjoy!
- Take time over your meals and really taste the food.
- Become aware of each person you communicate with and find at least one thing to appreciate about them.
- Be thankful for the beauty of the day.

This level of experience is intense and very uplifting. You may find that minutes and even hours go by when you forget to appreciate your day. As soon as you realize, just get back in there with your positive awareness and lift your experience again. Cultivate your appreciation for just one day and see where it leads you. All things are indeed bright and beautiful but we need to develop our gratitude for life before we can truly appreciate this. Optimism and positivity are fabulous tools and they arise from gratitude and appreciation. Appreciate just for today and maybe you will feel like doing it again tomorrow.

Reflections

- It's not *what* happens to you that counts but how you deal with what happens to you.
- Grumpy people really do have a miserable life: they give out negativity and so they attract more negativity.
- Positive thinking attracts positive things into your life; use this powerful tool and watch it transform your experiences.
- Love life and it will love you back. Just give it a try!
- Find something to appreciate in everyone you meet.
- Every day of your life is a miracle.

19

Where Are You Going and Why?

'Our purpose is to be. Our purpose is how we live life, not what role we live. Our purpose is found each moment as we make choices to be who we really are.'

CAROL ADRIENNE

When I watch my granddaughter running around, investigating anything and everything, expressing all her needs as she feels them and saying whatever comes into her head, I know that she knows without a doubt who she really is. Guileless, innocent, pleasure-loving, vulnerable and free, she loves herself and her world with passion and without question. Such is life through the senses of a two-year-old. Of course, as she learns more of the world and its ways, and begins to understand the rules of society, her open-eyed wonder and natural sense of self will start to fade.

There is more to all this than meets the eye

When we start to ask meaningful questions about life (why are we here? who am I? what is my purpose?) it's good to remember that once upon a time we knew all these answers. We knew them instinctively, in our bones and in our hearts: we have all been two years old.

Years can pass during which we remain oblivious to the deeper meaning of life. Oh, we appear to be getting ourselves together – passing exams, getting a job, having relationships – and it all *seems* OK on the surface, but somehow there's a sense of something missing. This feeling of lack of fulfilment can act like a wake-up call and lead us on to a journey of self-discovery as we begin our search for 'something more' in our lives. And it seems that at that very moment of awakening we step onto a new path where life is never quite the same again.

This path is no bed of roses, and we can get a lot of flak from some of those around us who may think we: are utterly self-absorbed/nutty as a fruitcake/suffering from delusions/clueless about how the world really works ... Although I'm speaking light-heartedly here, I do know that sometimes it can feel hard to pursue this path and doubts may arise. But you *are* right: there is more to you than meets the eye; it is the apparent superficiality of life that is the illusion. You are powerful, strong and utterly amazing; just believe this.

Our new awareness (of this vast personal potential) inevitably leads us onwards in a quest to discover how we can tap into and access these inner resources. How can we step into our own greatness? Questions arise: what exactly am I trying to achieve? Is this the best I can do? Do I feel underused or under-valued (or both)? Am I going in the right direction? Take time now to consider where you might be going and why.

Are you happy with the way your life is going? Do your relationships support you? Do you feel purposeful and optimistic most of the time? Do you enjoy the work you do? Would you like to make changes in your life?

Is it time to move on?

Dissatisfaction is a natural feeling and can be put to use in a positive way. When we are discontented we are naturally inclined to look for someone to blame. But the blame game is for victims; we can only change a situation once we accept the responsibility for our part in helping to create it. So rather than fall into that negative cycle of despair, blame and inertia, why not take a more positive approach and let your discontent be your guide.

Life is all about change, and as we develop and grow we are playing a part in this natural process. You know how this works. Think of a time in the past when you were happy with a certain aspect of your life (relationship, job or whatever) and then your feelings changed and somehow things just didn't feel right any more. Your dissatisfaction was a sign that you had outgrown this particular situation and were ready to move on. We change continually and what was perfect last year (or even last week) may be far from perfect now. Be ready to look into your own eyes and make a realistic assessment of where you are at. If you are feeling less than satisfied, this is a clear sign that something needs to change. Ask yourself some big questions and let your answers be big! Be expansive, express your real needs and desires, and get in touch with your own truth.

Looking into your own eyes

Now ask yourself these questions:

1. What do I really want to do with my life?

2. What gifts do I bring?

3. How can I develop my unique skills and strengths?

4. Can I trust myself, and if not, why not?

5. What are my greatest fears when I think about making changes?

6. What is the first step I need to take to get myself moving again?

Moving out of your comfort zone

This exercise may have left you feeling uncomfortable. We are such creatures of habit and we love the familiarity of our routines because it helps us to feel secure. But our true self is bigger than our habits: the part of us that is drawn to self-change will never be lulled into a false sense of security for very long. Whenever you outgrow your comfort zone it is time to make changes. You will always recognize this feeling, which has been called divine discontent.

After the first flush of inspired wisdom and rush of excitement about the *idea* of change, there sometimes comes a more testing time: things are not what they were; we can't rely on our past structures and the new systems are not yet in place. It can feel as though the carpet has been pulled from under our feet; what once seemed secure is now uncertain and we may start wishing that we had let things stay as they were.

Whenever you are caught between the old and the new,

remind yourself that your purpose is to be true to yourself. You are caught in this moment and you cannot see the bigger picture of your life, but every little decision and action that you take has implications further down the line.

EXERCISE:

Waiting for the mist to clear

Imagine that you are standing on a mountaintop surrounded by a swirling mist. You can only see what is very close to you; the rest is hidden. But you know that a beautiful landscape stretches for miles all around you. As the mist starts to clear you see more and more of the spectacular scenery: the mountain streams becoming a river which flows through the valley, the path ahead leading down to a small hamlet below, the cows grazing on the lush grass in the far distance, the birds flying overhead, and the road passing through the valley which eventually leads out to the city.

Whenever you are feeling alone and isolated you are experiencing an illusion. You cannot see the way ahead because you cannot see the bigger picture. When the time is right you will see your way forward and you will also find the connections that you are looking for; you are only waiting for the mist to clear.

Keep your nerve as you let go of the old and await the new. Remember that your true purpose is found in each moment as you make choices about who you really are. Be true to yourself and choose well; you have the power and the resolve to do this.

Reflections

- Our purpose is *how* we live and not what role we live.
- When you were tiny you had a natural sense of your true self.
- You are powerful, strong and utterly amazing; just believe this.
- You are not alone; you are only waiting for the mist to clear.
- What gifts do you bring?
- Be prepared to step into your own greatness.

20

De-junk Your Life

'Have nothing in your homes that you do not know to be useful and believe to be beautiful.'

Well, I must come clean here and admit that Life Laundry has not been one of my greatest strengths. The only times I have ever been really riveted by cleaning and ordering were in the pre-labour hours before each of my three children were born. I have a weakness for hoarding 'things that might come in handy' and books and magazines that I 'might read one day'. In the past, each room in our house had a junk drawer or cupboard, and I only ever opened them to throw something in. But I'm happy to say that I'm becoming a convert to de-cluttering, because it makes me feel so good and virtuous and liberated!

When the spare room was so full of useless tat that I couldn't open the door any more, I took a reluctant trip to the municipal dump. And what a place for instant catharsis! I drove in with a car full of rubbish and 15 minutes later I was a free woman (feeling spiritually, physically and emotionally uplifted). There is no doubt that collecting and hoarding the non-beautiful and the non-useful just weighs us down physically and psychologically.

If you get up in the morning to domestic civility, this chapter is probably not for you. But for the more chaotic among us (you know who you are) there is hope! If you can never find anything clean to wear, your paperwork is sitting in assorted cardboard boxes, the floor of the car is covered in sweet wrappers, you have more than one clutter hotspot in your house, or you have any variations on these themes, it's time to bring some order into your life.

Overcoming domestic chaos

The only way to approach de-junking is easily, slowly and methodically. Take a good look around you and list clutter hotspots such as piles of magazines/clothes/books/toys, junk drawers/boxes/closets, mayhem under the bed/on top of the wardrobe. Go from room to room and write down the specific areas that need clearing. Whatever you do, don't allow yourself to become overwhelmed by it all so that you give up before you start. Plan your de-junking campaign realistically. Do one small job at a time and then cross it off your list. As you begin to create new space around you, your self-respect will reach dizzying heights.

EXERCISE:

Use it or lose it

This isn't as drastic as it sounds because there really are three 'use it' categories: the useful, the beautiful and the sentimental. Collect some cardboard boxes and begin! As you evaluate each article ask yourself these questions. Is it beautiful? Is it useful? Does it have sentimental value? The first two are easy to decide, but watch this last one. Are you sure you absolutely can't live without this item or is this nostalgic streak the very one that is creating your clutter problem? Be ruthless and decisive or you will never get to lose anything. And don't sabotage yourself by tackling too much at once so that you bury yourself in 'stuff' and end up just throwing it all back into new piles. Once you have cleared an area, stop and rest and do some more another day. Gradually you will fill boxes for the rubbish dump or for recycling and maybe for the charity shop. Don't forget that someone else may really value something that is no longer of any use to you. Pass things on to people who will appreciate them and use them (this is true recycling).

Letting go of the old and receiving the new

If our lives are cluttered with material objects we feel psychologically crowded, with no space to think and relax. We can bring order out of chaos by simplifying the way that we live, and this leads to an increase in mental clarity and lowers our stress levels.

An ancient universal law states that to bring more abundance into our lives we first have to create room to receive this new prosperity. While we hang on to the redundant and useless articles that surround us we are metaphysically hanging on to old energy patterns and past limitations. Take that closet full of clothes for example. Why are you keeping items that you never wear and know for sure you will never wear again? Check out your sentimental attachment to that old skirt/coat/bag, etc. And why are you keeping that dress that was always too small for you? Every time you look at clothes that don't fit you and never will, you undermine your body confidence (it's enough to make you reach for the biscuit tin). Don't let the past hold you back; if you haven't worn something for the last three years, do you really think you ever will? What future are you waiting for that includes the relics of the past?

The process of change always requires that we let go of some part of ourselves that no longer serves us, in order to step into our new ways of being. This psychological process is mirrored at the physical level: how can we welcome the new and the good if we have nowhere to put it?

Emotional spring cleaning

Bringing order to the material world can lead directly to a desire for psychological clarity. Look at the places where you are most stretched and stressed. What can you do to streamline your life so that you are not under such pressure? A more manageable house, clothes laid out for the morning and some time management will certainly lessen the strain of everyday life. But authentic outer order comes from a real sense of inner order, and this is not only about list-making and keeping things together. An obsession with cleaning and ordering does not lead to emotional clarity; as with everything, balance is the key. Do what needs to be done to make space in your life (physically and emotionally) and then take some of that space for yourself. Take time to reflect on your day and do this regularly. Clear your mind and tap into your inner needs. Self-awareness will increase your confidence levels and lead to a sense of inner order and tranquillity. Make space in your cupboards and make space in your mind and you will feel clear, uplifted and in control.

Reflections

- As you simplify the way you live you will increase your mental clarity and lower your stress levels.
- To bring abundance into our lives we must first create the space to receive it.
- While we hang on to redundant articles we are metaphysically hanging on to old energy patterns and limitations.
- How can you welcome the new and the good if you have no room to put it in?
- Authentic outer order comes from a real sense of inner order.
- Make space in your life both physically and emotionally and you will feel clear, uplifted and in control.

21

Go With the Flow

You are not enclosed within your
bodies,

nor confined to houses or fields.

That which is you dwells above the
mountain

and roves with the wind.

It is not a thing that crawls into the
sun for warmth

or digs holes into darkness for safety,

But a thing free, a spirit that envelops
the earth

and moves in the ether.

KAHLIL GIBRAN

Standing at the sink/cooker/washing machine, it may well be
very hard to believe that who you really are is not confined to

the house, let alone that you are not enclosed within your body. If your spirit is free, then why do you feel so trapped?

Worldly business engages you mentally, physically and emotionally: you respond to the ups and downs in your life by thinking, feeling and doing. If you want to 'dwell above the mountain', 'rove with the wind' and step out of the daily round, you only need to tap into the universal energy source.

Becoming a creative channel

In her wonderful book *Living in the Light*, Shakti Gawain describes what it means to become a creative channel. She says: 'When you willingly follow where your creative energy leads, the higher power can come through you to manifest its creative work. When this happens, you will find yourself flowing with the energy, doing what you really want to do, and feeling the power of the universe moving through you to create or transform everything you do.'

Being a channel simply means that you are in touch with that place within you where your spiritual self (or Higher Self) connects with the highest creativity of the universe. Although this may sound very remote and hard to understand, I guarantee that you have experienced this connection many times.

If you have *ever* felt inspired or enthusiastic about *anything* you have been a creative channel. These qualities are the hallmark of the activities of your Higher Self and so you can always tell when you are coming from the highest source. Think of a time when you felt full of inspiration and enthusiasm. Go back into the experience, visualizing it as clearly as possible. What was the situation? How did your energy feel?

When you are acting as a creative channel for universal energy, your spirit reaches for the very highest within you and you feel amazing. Whenever you are truly inspired by some-thing – a piece of music, a beautiful rose, a new project, a workout at the gym, an exciting new relationship – your spiri-tual energy is at work, uplifting, harmonizing, expanding, calming and centring you. The word 'inspire' is connected to the word 'spirit', and your spiritual energy is light and free because it is linked to the universal energy flow. So we know how great it feels to be inspired and maybe we can remember the last time we felt like this, but how do we get to keep this dynamic, exciting, enlivening and elevating feeling?

You have acted as a channel many times in your life but you have probably done so unconsciously. A friend of mine who goes for a long run very early every morning can't understand why everyone isn't out there pounding the inner-city pavements at 5 am. He says, 'When I get home from my morning run I feel so good that I could jump right over my house.' Now, this man is a keen athlete and knows how to increase his feel-good endorphin and oxygen levels, and so if I told him that he was acting as a creative channel for the energy of the universe every morning I know he would look at me most strangely! But he would be the first to admit that he is pretty high on life and I know that his fitness activities are beginning to have a profound effect on the way he sees himself.

In other words, this spiritual connection is not dependent upon hours of meditation, solitude, a solemn face and a strict diet. Your Higher Self is busy appreciating life, sending you intuitive messages and injecting large amounts of grace into your life at every moment of the day; you just need to become conscious of this.

Choosing to become aware

Step 1

Stop, just for a moment. Put the book down, close your eyes and relax. Imagine that universal energy is pouring into your body and filling you with light, grace and power. Accept these gifts with silent thanks. Open your eyes and imagine that you are in a state of grace, because you are!

Don't worry if you don't feel amazing after doing this visualization. As you choose to increase your awareness you will experience more and more of your innate spirituality.

Step 2

Let's look at any of the things that could be standing in the way of your spiritual development. Make a list of anything that might be holding you back.

Here is a list of some of the most common fears that people feel when they first begin their spiritual quest:

- I don't believe in God so how can I qualify for a spiritual experience?

- It all sounds a bit New Ageish and cranky.

- My friends might laugh at me if they knew what I was trying to do.

- What if I can't do it?

- My partner would think that I am really cracking up.

- I'm afraid of revealing my insecurities.

- I like to place my bets on what I can see in front of me; how can I trust an invisible world?

- How can I know that what I feel is real; maybe it's all in my imagination?

- If this is going to be about religion, I'm not interested.

Remember that you are mind, body, *spirit* and emotions. Your spiritual energy exists. It is real and has nothing to do with your beliefs about God or any religion. Whether you believe in God or not, you are still a child of the universe. Whether you belong to a particular religious faith or not, you still have a Higher Self. If you are worried about the reactions of others or fear trusting the process of your development, just relax and know that you are connected to divine energy and your connection will lead you to make all the right moves.

The spiritual teacher Ramakrishna tells us that when a tree is a tiny sapling we protect it from animals by surrounding it with a fence. Later, when the tree has grown, it has no need for the fence and can then itself give protection as well as shelter to many. And so it is with spiritual growth. At first we are full of questions, our faith is shaky and we may feel vulnerable. Protect yourself by discussing spiritual issues only with others who are also interested. When you are feeling spiritually stronger (it won't take long) you won't need to safeguard yourself in this way. In fact, before long you will find that others will want to know about your inner experiences. There is no risk involved; choose to become aware and experience your divine connection.

Reflections

- Your spirit is free; decide to experience this.
- When our spiritual growth feels like a tiny sapling, we need to protect ourselves until we are spiritually strong and powerfully rooted.
- Becoming a creative channel will change your life; the power of the universe will transform all that you do and you will be going with the flow.
- You have experienced your Higher Self many times in your life; you just need to become consciously aware of this.
- When we are full of inspiration and enthusiasm we are experiencing a connection with divine energy.
- You are always in a state of grace (even when it doesn't feel as if you are).

22

Not Such an Ugly
Duckling

*'Always be a first-rate version of
yourself, instead of a second-rate
version of someone else.'*

JUDY GARLAND

Down on the duck pond there's a strange creature with a long neck, who has feathers that are stubby and brown, and he just *cannot* fit in with the rest of the ducks however hard he tries. He can't walk like them, talk like them or even swim like them, and despite his best efforts he *always* feels like a second-rate duckling. That is, until the happy day when the cygnet turns into an elegant swan and realizes that he has been pointlessly trying to be something that he could never ever be.

If you have ever felt strange or different, that your life doesn't seem to fit you properly, that you have to pretend to blend in, you will recognize this alienating sense of 'otherness'. Even if you don't feel like a stranger in a strange land, you may still experience a sense of not really knowing who you are or what you want from life. Or maybe you have felt restricted and limited at times, like a caterpillar in a cocoon that longs to emerge as a beautiful butterfly? All of these experiences are quite natural and common, so you can stop worrying that you are unusually preoccupied; we all wrestle with the demons of self-doubt and insecurity.

You are a one-off, utterly unique and totally original, and this is how you entered the world. But inevitably some of your originality has been tamed out of you; the socialization process has dampened your unique spirit and smoothed out your most unacceptable creases. Many of your natural creative gifts may have been lost or buried in your childhood. Negative words are so inhibiting: *Oh, you really are hopeless. Why are you always so slow? What a racket! You really have no musical ear. You can't possibly dance with flat feet like yours. You call that painting? What on earth is it supposed to be? You are definitely not a creative type.*

We have all internalized many of the messages that we heard in early childhood, and these have become the beliefs that circumscribe our life. Although most of us have many more negative than positive self-beliefs, this is no reason to feel dejected. The fabulous news is that our beliefs can be changed and that we can do this easily!

EXERCISE:

When you were a child

Go back to your childhood and think about some of the things you loved to do. What sort of child were you? What were your natural talents? Did you feel limited in any way? Finish the following statements.

When I was a child:

I always loved to . . . .

I was interested in . . . .

At school I felt . . . .

My friendships were . . . .

My parents thought that creativity was . . . .

I remember feeling really great when . . . .

I wanted to be . . . .

My teachers made me feel . . . .

My family life was . . . .

I thought I was . . . .

I felt as if . . . .

My imagination was . . . .

I always wanted to . . . .

I wasn't allowed to . . . .

My parents didn't like me to . . . .

My best memories of this time are . . . .

This exercise may take some thinking about. You may need to let your memories simmer for a few days before recollections can emerge. Is there anything here that reveals your authentic childhood self? Are there any negative beliefs and ideas that may have affected you? Was your creativity encouraged or curtailed? Did you ever get to do what you were longing to do, or were you often disappointed? Can you remember ever trying to fit in or be 'normal' in some way? Were you ever encouraged to display your natural talents or were you steered into the mainstream?

I wonder if you can recall a childhood passion that was never enacted. You may have longed for ballet lessons, which your parents couldn't afford. Or maybe you wanted to learn to play the piano and it was out of the question. Further on down the line you may have been inspired to act, or paint, or write poetry, and your parents (afraid for your future) would only support a vocational degree or an accountancy qualification. Did you become a teacher because it was your father's dream? Perhaps you fulfilled your parents' wishes and can now feel your own desires sprouting through your veneer.

Dismantling your false ceilings

If you feel dissatisfied about anything in your life, you have the power to change it. Remember that indomitable will and creative spirit that you brought with you to the planet? You still have these strengths; you only need to find them. Look into your past for the clues that you need to change your future. And then let go of any limitations that you discover; there are no limits unless you believe there are!

Our caretakers (parents, teachers, etc.), often with the best will in the world, may have helped us to create a set of artificially low false ceilings, which will always stop us reaching the heights. These self-limiting beliefs and ideas can be changed. Yes, you *can* do that! Of course you are clever enough to ... No, it's not too late to have riding lessons, go to art school, play the violin, take that exam, change your career path. Yes, you have many creative gifts – use them! You are not an ugly duckling, you are a beautiful swan.

Take a positive and inspired approach. Find out what is holding you back and then *leave it behind*. Let go of blame, recriminations and regret (all these will keep you stuck in your rut). Move forwards, follow your passions and make the very most of your life. Become a first-rate version of yourself.

Visualizing the real you

Sit quietly, close your eyes and relax for a few moments. Now imagine that you are full of creativity and positivity. Feel the energy that this brings. See yourself being successful, happy and fulfilled. How do you look? What are you doing? Who are you doing it with? Play with your imagination and create some great scenarios. Make these imaginings as real as you can and include your sensory perceptions. Feel the atmosphere in the scenes, hear the noises, smell the smells, really *be there*. See the real you in full flow, with all the support and help you need. Recognize who you really are, and when you open your eyes know that you are already on the way to making your visualizations come true.

Reflections

- You are a one-off, utterly unique and totally original.
- Some of your greatest natural talents may have been lost or buried in your childhood.
- You can easily change any belief that is not working for you.
- Are you living someone else's dream?
- Look into the past to find the clues you need to change your future. And then *let go* of the past.
- Become a first-rate version of yourself.

23

Enjoying Your Work

*'Your work is to discover your work
and then with all your heart to give
yourself to it.'*

THE BUDDHA

An expert in workplace trends throws new light on the old
belief that work is necessarily pressurizing and anxiety-making.
The new research suggests that work has changed for the better
and that it has become more satisfying and fun and is an important part of our lives. There's not much doubt that it *is* an
important part of our lives, and given that we spend so much
time at work I suspect this has always been true. As for 'more
satisfying and fun', I just wonder about the notion of work
changing; surely it's only people who change!

When we go to work we take ourselves

The workplace is made up of people, and work is all about
relationships. If work becomes fun, it's because people have
made it fun and, if it's pressurizing, we – or our colleagues – are
making it so. We take ourselves wherever we go and we cannot
escape our own beliefs, attitudes, expectations and moods. It's
so easy to blame 'work' for our shortfalls (underachievement,

lack of money, boredom); if we act like a victim at work we can expect to be treated like one.

It's always hard to succeed at anything if you don't enjoy it, and maybe you don't like the work you do. Take a creative approach to your dilemma. If you are unfulfilled and feeling resentful, is there any way you can turn this around by changing your attitude? For example, if your salary supports you or your family perhaps you can find a sense of gratitude and appreciation for that? When you can love your work (for whatever reason) the energy will start moving again and you will begin to attract new opportunities – positive energy always attracts more of the same. And if you are fed up with work because you are longing for a different career, what are you doing to make this change happen? Do you need more training? Are you actively seeking new prospects? Are you networking and sending out copies of your CV?

EXERCISE:

Visualizing your dream job

Our negative beliefs, personal glass ceilings, low expectations and the pictures that we carry in our imagination create our own version of reality. When you can 'see' a new scenario in your mind's eye, you draw it into your real experience. Suspend your disbelief for five minutes, sit down, relax and close your eyes.

Imagine yourself in your dream job. Create your preferred environment and take a good look at the scene. See yourself working happily and feel your interest and liveliness. Be as creative as possible and include as much detail as you can imagine. Recreate this vision as often as possible.

You have now demonstrated your desires both to yourself and to the rest of the universe. Do what you need to do to make this vision a reality and know that the universe supports your every action.

Finding the balance

Of course our work is only one part of our life and sometimes it feels like part of a fairly impossible juggling act. Women are particularly brilliant at multi-tasking and once they join the world of work they can find themselves with at least two full-time jobs (and this really does require some organizational skills). Those of you with children know only too well that keeping it all going requires a miraculous performance. So as you grab a sandwich at lunchtime on your way to shop for your nearest and dearest, spare a thought for yourself.

The pressure of keeping everything together (throwing and catching all those balls) can often feel just too much. If this sounds like you, it's time to reassess and get your life into perspective. You can only give what you have, and if your goodwill and energy run out, everything comes to a standstill. Put your health and wellbeing first; if you burn out the game is over. Try the following tips to help you create a happier and more balanced lifestyle.

Eight tips for balancing work and home

1. **Prioritize yourself!** Schedule free time for doing nothing, even if you are surrounded by chaos.
2. **Learn to settle for a less than perfect home.** Domestic jobs just keep on coming; accept this and stop trying always to keep on top.
3. **Delegate household tasks,** make a list of jobs for everyone and make sure they do them. This is as easy as it sounds (I've done it and it works a treat).
4. **Book some exercise time into your diary,** but don't take your foreign language tapes with you to the gym (practise doing one thing at a time).

5. Look at the bigger picture of your life: you are meant for greater things than meeting all those targets.

6. Take time to stand and stare; practise this and you will find the habit will grow on you.

7. When you just can't beat the clock, remember your sense of humour. Laughter brings things back into perspective.

8. Slow down: your breathing, your talking, your pace. Take time to appreciate your precious life.

You are only as stressed as you believe you are

It's all the rage to be stressed, but stress always lies in the eye of the beholder. When life at work starts getting to you, don't let yourself become a 'stress victim' who blames their job for all their negative mental states. Use a positive mental approach to deal with difficult work scenarios and keep your mood upbeat and friendly. And remember, if after all this effort you are still feeling pressurized, it might be worth considering a career change!

10 ways to be happy at work

1. Stop using the 'stress' label. If work life is troublesome, understand the difficulties and then try to resolve them.

2. Be specific about the problems and name them; it then becomes easier to find solutions.

3. Discuss your situation with a trusted friend; constructive feedback may bring new insights.

4. Don't moan or gossip; this path leads to a negative place.

5. Use good communication skills to express your needs assertively.

6. Don't let yourself be victimized by others. Whenever you act like a victim, others will treat you like one.

7. Think of your work problems as challenges that you can overcome.

8. Use a creative approach to problem-solving.

9. Keep positive and confident and people will treat you with respect.

10. Take your spirituality to the workplace. You are a spiritual being even at work! Use your intuitive awareness and natural empathy and kindness and you will be amazed by the way that others respond.

Reflections

- When you can 'see' a new scenario in your mind's eye you draw it into your real experience.
- Schedule free time for yourself.
- Keep your sense of humour.
- Always use a positive mental approach when dealing with difficult work scenarios.
- Use a creative and inspired approach to problem solving.
- When you can love your work you begin to attract all sorts of new opportunities.

24

Awakening Your Soul

Soul 1. the spirit or immaterial part of man, the seat of human personality, intellect, will and emotions, regarded as an entity that survives the body after death.

COLLINS ENGLISH DICTIONARY

The 'immaterial part of man': what does this definition mean to you? What do we mean when we talk about 'soul music', 'soul food', 'the life and soul of the party', 'a soulful mood', 'lost souls' ...? What part of you is your soul; where is it and are you aware of it?

In her book *Bridge of Light,* LaUna Huffines makes a clear distinction between our soul and our personality by using the beautiful analogy of a mountain stream. Imagine snow falling on top of the highest mountain. The snow is pure and its brilliance reflects the light of the sun. As some of this snow melts, it creates waterfalls and streams that flow into the valley below. And as these streams go rushing down the mountainside, getting further from their source, they gather more and more debris until they lose their original sweetness and clarity. The river depends upon the constant flow of fresh water from the melting snow, and whenever the river becomes blocked upstream it relies on the sparkling waters of the newly melted snow to flush the channel clear again. Just as the snow is the source of the mountain streams, so your soul is the source of your life force.

Visualize these streams as elements of your personality (mind/body/emotions) that come together to create a powerful and unified personality. Of course the muddied streams (having gathered everything in their path) and the resulting river are now much more than pure melted snow. In the same way our personality has collected all it has learned from the world and so its energy streams contain much more than the 'pure spirit' with which our life journey began.

Gold stars are not enough

Deep within us, permeating every cell, is who we really are – our core, our soul, our essence. This image of a formless essence that is beyond, behind and beneath our personality is a concept that is hard to grasp. The energy streams that create our personality contain all sorts of limiting debris that we can find hard to recognize as our river rushes on. As our personal flotsam and jetsam bobs in and out of our lives we are more inclined to rush on through than to pick out these bits and pieces of self-limiting, useless clutter.

Achievement, success and worldly gain are personality goals that have public approval, and our personality always likes to be awarded gold stars. But as we know, bucketfuls of worldly success do not necessarily create happiness and contentment. The pure snow of the mountain stream is still present in the mature river; the river depends on it for continuous flow. In the same way we depend upon our 'pure spirit' (soul) to continually infuse our lives with clarity, true purpose and energy. When life is boring, you don't feel 'good enough', shopping/chocolate/sex do not uplift you, you feel as if you've lost track and depression means much, much more than a bad hair day ... it is time to awaken your soul.

Your essential blueprint

Think of your soul as the essential blueprint of who you really are. William Bloom says that it carries 'the pattern for your perfect fulfilment'. So your soul knows your mission – the reason why you are here on the planet – and it will not let you go in peace when you take a path that is not true for you.

We have seen how we can rise above our personality to make contact with the spiritual world and so become our Higher Selves. And it is through this most highly developed part of you, your Higher Self, that your soul is able to fulfil its purpose. When you are acting from your Higher Self you are carrying out the plans of your soul, not following the needs and desires of your personality. Again, don't get lost by trying to understand these concepts: thought will keep you at a personality level. Open your mind to the awareness of your soul. Try the following exercises and see what you experience.

EXERCISE:

Make your own mission statement

Step 1
Your soul contains the essence of who you are and why you came to the planet, and whenever your life doesn't ring true to the original plan your soul knows it. What does your blueprint hold? What are the amazing and unique qualities, abilities and strengths that you have brought with you into this world? These

questions are hard to answer from the standpoint of our (worldly) personality, which is largely motivated by the desire to succeed in earthly matters. But remember how the continuous flow of the river depends upon the fresh, sparkling waters of newly melted snow. Remember how your personality also depends upon the pure spirit of your soul to continually give meaning, purpose and vision to your life.

Writing and developing your own personal mission statement requires that you think about yourself in a new way. Answer the following questions and write down your answers.

1. What is it that you do that makes a difference to people and to humanity? . . . .

2. What motivates you to do the things that you think are important? . . . .

3. Why do you do the things you do? . . . .
. . . .

4. What is of greatest value to you in your life? . . . .
. . . .

If we judge our lifestyle by the dictates of our personality, these questions will be very hard to answer. We need to look at ourselves and the meaning of our life in a completely different way; we need to look at the larger picture. Our life means so much more than we think it does. We rarely live at our highest level; we rarely reach our potential. Our souls know this and so, at a spiritual level, we know this, and that's why we so often feel unhappy and unfulfilled.

Step 2
Imagine being your Higher Self; visualize that bright shining jewel at the very centre of your being. Now think about those questions again, from this higher vibration. Yes, you are amazing! What

special strengths do you have that can help to make positive changes in your relationships and in your immediate environment? List your strengths.

. . . .

. . . .

. . . .

Well, what is your mission statement? What exactly is your life's purpose? Be sure to know that you do have a purpose or you wouldn't be here at this time and in this place. Why are you here? To make people laugh? To make sure that your children believe in themselves? To teach? To spread happiness? To raise money for worthy causes? To increase environmental awareness? To look after a sick child? To create beauty that others can enjoy? To love your family? To develop yourself spiritually? To reach for the stars and go beyond your limitations? To listen to others?

Your soul knows your potential and it is constantly reminding you. When you feel that you said the wrong thing to someone and want to go back to apologize, when you feel dissatisfied (a sure sign that you have lost direction), when a relationship is not working, these are all soul nudges, reminding you of your larger purpose and your true potential. Listen to your soul; all your questions have an answer if you can learn how to hear. Discover what really drives you from within and then match it with real-world activities to give your life new purpose and meaning.

Touch your soul

Here is a wonderful way to contact your shining essence.

Close your eyes and relax. Put you right hand over your heart and say to yourself, 'I breathe the soul's breath.'

Exhale and wait until your breath naturally comes to you to fill the space. When your breath comes to you in this way, you are breathing the soul's breath.

Enjoy this exercise and repeat it as often as you wish. Your soul contact will become stronger and stronger.

Reflections

- Your soul is pure spirit and is the source of your life.
- As soon as you become aware of your soul, its work with you changes and your spiritual development will accelerate.
- As our personalities develop, we become cluttered with worldly matters, but our soul is always waiting for our awareness so that it can re-inject our lives with clarity, meaning and joy.
- When we keep 'digging in the wrong place' our soul will try to let us know (we feel these messages as unhappiness, dissatisfaction, boredom etc.).
- We all come to this planet with a mission (or missions!). Keep reminding yourself of your true purpose and live at the highest level you can.
- Breathe the 'soul's breath' and touch your shining essence. You can do this anywhere at any time.

25

Because You're Worth It

'If someone wants to insult you, they might look at you and say, "Get a life!" This is not a bad thing to consider. It is only when you know that you don't have a life that the thought of trying to get one will freak you out!'

IYANLA VANZANT

Having a life means more than being alive and functioning on the planet. When you have a life you can own your experiences, make things happen, believe in yourself, know your own truth (and stand by it) and keep on keeping on (even when times are hard). To have a really good life you must respect yourself; this is the basic requirement. You must believe that you really are worth it!

Do you think and act as if you are worth:

- Defending
- Supporting
- Standing up for

- Nurturing
- Listening to
- Encouraging
- Rewarding
- Loving
- Appreciating?

Are you sinking or swimming?

Yes it really is time to get a life when you:

- Can't make decisions
- Have low self-worth
- Can't trust yourself
- Are in a relationship that is making you unhappy
- Feel like a victim
- Have lost faith in yourself and others
- Are stuck in blame/anger/hurt

If you suffer any of the above, there is a simple remedy. Your life can only ever be as good as you can let it be, and it's confidence that opens the door to love, joy, happiness and fulfilment – confidence in self, others and the process of life. But how can you lift your spirit and lighten your days when you find yourself in that negative spiral of low self-worth? How can you access that magical quality that will empower, support and sustain you through your daily ups and downs?

Quick Quiz – 10 things that give you confidence

Confidence depends upon self-knowledge; the more you know about the way you tick, the easier it will be to feel and act assertively. Stop dwelling on your weaknesses and start to concentrate on your strengths. When do you feel powerful and strong? Complete the following statements to find out exactly what does give you confidence.

1. I am at my best when ....

2. I feel really sexy when ....

3. I feel attractive when ....

4. My finest asset is ....

5. My personality strengths are ....

6. The most incredible thing I have ever done is ....

7. I feel empowered when ....

8. I love it when I ....

9. I am proud of myself for ....

10. The thing I like best about myself is ....

Look at your completed statements. What a fine description of a positive and motivated person! Confidence depends upon the way we see ourselves, and if we keep bringing ourselves down that is where we will stay – down. So keep looking to your strengths and increase your self-awareness and you will find that the life you live will become more and more fascinating.

Are your needs being met?

When you know that you are worth it (when you feel self-worth) you will find it easier to stand up for yourself in any situation. Increasing levels of confidence will inevitably lead you to a review of some of your relationships: the more you respect yourself the more you expect from your relationships. When your confidence is low you are much more likely to attract and settle for poor quality relationships which don't satisfy your needs. So as you change and become stronger, you may begin to question the nature of many of your relationships (including those with family, lovers, friends and colleagues).

Healthy relationships allow you to satisfy your basic needs and so leave you feeling free to be yourself. What are your needs in a relationship? What do you like? What can't you bear? How far are you prepared to go with someone else? Of course you will have different boundary lines with different people. Perhaps you tell your best friend things that you don't tell your partner; maybe you find it hard to open up to intimacy; trust may be an issue that limits how far you can go with others. Whatever your situation it can always be understood in terms of boundaries. A boundary, or limit, is the distance you can comfortably go in a relationship (it can be emotional, physical, mental, spiritual or any combination of these).

Once you become aware of your boundaries, you can really begin to get to know who you are and what you want, and until you begin to identify these things it will be impossible for you to know what is right and what is wrong for you in any relationship.

If you have ever felt overwhelmed by someone else's feelings or swamped by a partner in an intimate relationship, then you have let your personal boundaries become blurred. You may have experienced that feeling of not knowing whether you are doing something because you really want to or whether you are only agreeing because someone else wants to do it. Again, it's a question of boundaries. Until you know yourself you will not know where you end and the other person begins. Until you know that you are worth it, no one else will know! Check your personal boundaries.

EXERCISE:

Checking your personal boundaries *

Answer the following questions, using one of the following answers:

Untrue   Sometimes true   Often true   True

1. I put others' needs before my own.

2. I am good at making decisions.

3. I feel responsible for other people.

4. People seem to take me for granted.

5. I find it difficult to express my true feelings.

6. I seem to put a lot into my relationships and get very little back.

7. I am unable to speak my mind.

8. I feel used by other people.

9. I like to make others feel good.

10. I am not victimized by other people.

11. I am frightened by angry feelings.

12. I make relationships with people who are not good for me.

13. I am afraid to spend time alone.

14. Criticism really hurts me.

15. I do not stay in abusive relationships.

16. I don't trust myself.

17. I am very sensitive to the moods of others.

18. I find it difficult to keep a secret.

19. I can enjoy the successes of others.

20. I feel upset if other people are upset.

   * Taken from my book, *The Self-Esteem Workbook*

Think about how each of your answers affects the quality of your relationships. Pay special attention to the behaviour and feelings that you think create a problem in your interaction with others; these are the places where your boundaries are weak. Wherever you have a boundary problem you will also have low self-worth. Poor relationships, unhealthy boundaries and low confidence go hand in hand.

Get a grip on your life: check your boundaries and take responsibility for your own needs. The confident and powerful you knows exactly what you want and how to get it. If you feel as if you haven't got a life, just go out and get one.

Be confident and others will be confident in you.

Stand up for yourself and others will respect you.

Demonstrate self-worth and others will treat you as if you are worth it!

Reflections

- Self-respect is the basic requirement for a really good life.
- Do you act as if you are worth it?
- Your life can only ever be as good as you can let it be.
- Are your needs being met?
- Once you become aware of your own boundaries you will be able to identify what is right and what is wrong for you in any relationship.
- Until you know that you are worth it, no one else will know.

26

You Sexy Thing!

'I never feel sexy because I can't ever match up to the way that glamorous models and celebrities look. I would love to have the confidence to be happy with myself. I think this would help me to feel sexy.'

A CLIENT

Are you a hot sexy siren with a fabulous figure and all the time and money in the world to pamper yourself? Are you oozing sex appeal and body confidence? Do you arrive home from work full of zest and vitality, ready to jump into bed with your partner for a night of passionate lovemaking?

If you have answered yes to these questions, all the rest of us want to hear from you *immediately* with your hot tips and advice. Relax, the truth is that all of us real people struggle with our sexual confidence. And who can blame us? Sexy images are everywhere: perfect airbrushed bodies and faces surround us on TV, in magazines, on the tube, on the bus, wherever we go. The pressure is on to be a sex god/goddess as well as a partner/ cook/worker/mother/father/housecleaner/washerupper/ foodshopper/DIY expert and all the rest! How can we begin to compete with these unreal glossy images? And there is absolutely no point in even beginning to try.

The simple truth is that when you are feeling sexy, you look sexy: sexual confidence does not depend on how you think you look on the outside, but rather on how you feel about yourself on the inside. So how can we increase our sex-esteem?

Confidence is sexy

Self-confidence is the greatest aphrodisiac of all: know yourself, know what you want and never be afraid to ask for it. When you are feeling good, you are looking good, so build up your confidence and let it show in your posture and body language. Walk tall, hold your head high and look and act assertively (this will soon become a habit even if it feels as if you are faking it at first).

The majority of people are dissatisfied with the way their bodies look, hence the massive growth in the diet and health and fitness industries. Don't buy into a negative self-image cycle or it will ruin your happiness. The cycle goes like this: I hate the way my ... looks ➔ If only I can lose weight/change my shape/look like ... I will be happy ➔ I hate the way my ... looks, etc. When you hate any part of your body and when you believe your happiness depends on physical changes, you are caught in a cycle of low self-esteem and low confidence. Step out of this cycle. Remember your true worth. Don't forget who you really are and all the great qualities and strengths that you bring to your life.

Learn to love your body, even if this seems impossible at first. Start by admiring a small piece of you (for example your fingernail) and then move on gradually to the rest. You won't be able to love your body if you are holding an image of some perfect beauty in your mind, so let go of this illusory competitor against whom you are evaluating your credentials. Learn to be happy in your own skin and your body confidence and sex-esteem will hit the roof.

Know your own sexual desires

Inner confidence, body confidence and sex-esteem are all connected. Being happy in your own skin means being at ease with who you are and being able to accept yourself (flabby bits and all). Although it isn't always easy to like ourselves, we can learn to be more in touch with our desires and our bodily senses and in this way we can get to know our own sexual chemistry (what turns us on and off). Men have traditionally led the field in this area, and women have taken a more passive role. But it's a long time since women were taught to lie back and think of England; now we are much more likely to be engaged in our own sexual fantasies. With shelves of books of female erotica, and sexy and sensual clothes and accessories readily available, there is no excuse for us to be inhibited about our own sexual desires.

There are some major differences between men and women in the realm of sexuality (excluding the obvious ones). Most men think about sex most of the time! And most women don't! If you are a woman and your sexuality is in the doldrums, just try this technique: start thinking about sex. It really works. The more you think about it, the more sexual you will feel. Don't be shy about admiring men's bodies or indulging in erotic fantasies; these activities are perfectly harmless and natural, and can lead to increased sexual awareness.

Releasing your inner sex goddess

Increase your sexual feelings by becoming more sensual in every part of your life.

- Wear silk underwear (or no underwear!). This will always add a dash to your day!

- Indulge in long steamy fragrant baths (alone or accompanied).

- Buy exotic perfume and lotions and potions.

- Read female erotica (to be found in all good bookshops).

- Pamper your body and tend to it with love and care.

- Read about sexual techniques and tips to create romance.

- Indulge yourself in your favourite edible treat.

- Be romantic and sexually assertive.

- Think and talk about sex (to your friends).

Get those sexy hormones racing

Most couples in a long-term relationship start to forget that they need to focus on their relationship in order to keep it fascinating and exciting. And we all know what happens to our sex life when we don't pay it attention! When our sexual relationship is neglected, the rest soon falls apart – be warned! Keep your sex life buzzing and your relationship will keep buzzing.

I know, there's no time, and there's the children, and you are both so tired all the time. But think of it this way: you deserve personal attention and sexual excitement and you deserve to feel sensual and desired, so take steps to spice things up a bit. Make time and space for sex, even if you have to book it into your diaries. Share your erotic fantasies and go shopping for sexy items together (this is a great turn on). Create a sensual atmosphere with candles and scented oils and let yourselves get in the mood. Don't do what you always do in that order! Experiment, be different and the excitement will increase. You have nothing to lose except your inhibitions, so go to it!

Reflections

- Sexual confidence does not depend on how you look on the outside but rather on how you feel about yourself on the inside.
- Self-confidence is the greatest aphrodisiac of all.
- Learn to be happy in your own skin and your body confidence and sex-esteem will hit the roof.
- Release your inner sex goddess by bringing sensuality into your life.
- Make time and space for sex and give it your full attention!
- You have nothing to lose except your inhibitions.

27

Focus on Dreamtime

'For more than 40,000 known years, Aborigines have walked in Dreamtime. In this "timeless" dimension, they dream towards the future and the future dreams back. In this realm, they alter the future by altering the way they dream back at it. We can do the same thing.'

JULIA CAMERON

Cast your mind back to your schooldays and think of the most boring teacher you were ever forced to endure. Imagine yourself back there in their class, suffering the dullest lesson in the world. The teacher is droning on and on and you are ... What are you doing? You are looking out of the window, drifting off into a space where you can't hear the teacher and you forget you are in a classroom. You are daydreaming; you are travelling in Dreamtime. This is a place where we can connect with the universal energy of the planet. We could think of this energy as an electrical power source that we can plug into at any time to switch ourselves on. And when we do connect in this way we can truly feel the current of spirituality coursing through us. Unfocused daydreaming is pleasant and relaxing, whereas focused daydreaming does the business!

Your imagination is the key

Circumstances, opportunities and people walk through the doors of our expectations. In other words, *what we believe is what we get* or, to put it another way, *we attract what we think about.* We have looked at these themes throughout this book, but now let's go to the roots of *how* we believe, expect and attract. We use the phrase 'seeing is believing' to mean that once we can see something in reality then we can believe in it. But this phrase actually expresses a universal law of creativity: *we see first and then we believe.* This means that whatever we continually imagine or see in our mind's eye will eventually materialize in some way in our world. This may be hard for our rational selves to accept, but just think, you use this process to create your life every moment of the day. Your breakfast was an idea and a vision before you made it and ate it. The room you are sitting in was once an idea in an architect's mind. Your plan to buy a great new outfit was an idea and a visualization that *took shape* in your mind's eye before you actually got to wear that stylish designer number. *Everything* that you do you have thought of and envisioned first, even if you have not been aware of it. You have been using your natural power of imagination, which is the basic creative energy of the universe. Whenever we create something we have always first had an idea (thought form), which then creates an image (visualization). The idea and the image create a blueprint that begins to magnetize and attract the necessary physical energies to manifest our original idea in physical form.

And so, back to Dreamtime. The power of our *imagination* together with our *desire to* make something happen (this desire is the energizing force) creates our personal reality:

That poor relationship you find yourself in is a result of unfocused or negative imaginative powers of the past. Do you want a great relationship? Then start to take Dreamtime seriously.

Are you unhappy in your job? Ask yourself why you have imagined and created this situation. Were your expectations for yourself too low? What new expectations could you start imagining for yourself?

Do you feel as if you are reaching your full potential? If not, what exactly are the negative images of yourself that are holding you back. There is no glass ceiling unless you imagine that there is!

Imagination, belief and expectations certainly create the characters and circumstances that emerge in our lives.

Albert Einstein said that, 'Imagination is more important than knowledge.' And here speaks a man who should know! It seems that all those long hours spent staring into space during my Latin lessons, wishing I wasn't there, could have been put to more constructive use.

You can *draw* your positive dreams out of Dreamtime and into reality by focusing on the outcome you desire. All you have to do to tap into this magical process is to change the negative and limiting pictures in your mind. Often, when opportunity knocks, we let self-doubt interfere; we think, 'I couldn't do that' and we actually *see* ourselves failing. Small wonder that we walk away from so many lucky breaks! So next time someone suggests you take on an exciting new project, just say yes and immediately *see* yourself doing a great job.

To enter this timeless dimension where we can alter our future by the way that we 'dream back at it' we need to set our imaginations free. Our imagination is a spiritual gift that we bring with us at birth and it makes our lives stimulating and creative (just watch a young child at play). As we grow (and learn to play by the rules) we begin to abandon our rich, imaginary life, but we still have this incredible creative tool buried beneath our layers of rationality. Excavate and discover the amazing power of your imagination.

EXERCISE:

Acting 'as if'

At first it may feel as if playing with imaginative ideas is a bit like make-believe – and it is! This doesn't make the process any less meaningful or productive; in fact the more playful and light you can be, the more powerfully your imagination can work. Suspend any disbelief, change the pictures in your mind and just see how this amazing process works.

Take any difficult personal problem and think it through. You will have done this unconsciously many times before as you tried to make some sense of your dilemma. Now act it out in your mind yet again, creating an inner movie complete with characters and dialogue, and make it a colourful, sensory experience (add smells, noises, voices, feelings ... whatever is appropriate). Now really let this movie run. Each time we replay an experience in this way we confirm its future reality (we dream it to happen in the future). Just think how many times we have played negative re-runs in our head, only to ensure that something very similar or the same will happen again. What can you do to break this cycle?

Stop all negative inner movies about this problem. This is the most important thing you can do. It may take a while for you to become aware of your constant gloomy imaginings, but you will gradually become more and more conscious of them.

Think through a new scenario where the characters do what you want them to do, or write them out of the plot. Put yourself in the play and give yourself all the confidence, skills and abilities that you need to provide a positive outcome.

Now create the new play in your head. Make everything as bright and as real as possible. Include a soundtrack and use only the words that you want to hear. If it's difficult to create a new script, just take some time out to answer such questions as what would I like to happen here? Who do I want to spend time with? What sort of person can I be? How would I feel if I realized my dreams?

Answer your big important questions and then act out 'as if' scenarios in your mind. Be sure to include yourself and as much detail as possible. Change the quality of your imaginings and experience the change in your life. Stick at this activity, keep the process as playful as possible and dream yourself a new future. Don't worry if this all feels a bit beyond you; keep a light-hearted mood and watch for positive changes.

Moving into your imagination

One of the most easy and enjoyable ways to move into our imaginative processes is actually to move *physically*. We are whole beings and when we move our energy at any one level (mind, body, spirit or emotions) this has a knock-on effect. The Aborigines *walk* into Dreamtime. This rhythmic process frees up the creative part of the brain. Try *walking out* your problems. Take your difficult decisions on a walk; step by step your awareness will change. There is no need to concentrate as you walk, just be aware that your inner processes are busy working things out as you enjoy the beat of your footfall on the grass, sand or concrete. Know that you will return with new ideas and solutions. Or you can cycle your way into this state, or jog, or swim or dance ... whatever you choose to do, make sure that you do it regularly.

Free your mind, step into Dreamtime and let your imagination create new and exciting realities. Whatever you see in your mind's eye will eventually be what you get, so make sure you imagine the very best for yourself.

Reflections

- The energy of the universe is a power source that you can plug into at any time. You can connect with this energy in Dreamtime.
- Focused daydreaming (imagination x desire) creates your personal reality.
- People and events walk through the doors of your expectations.
- Act 'as if' and make believe, and you will enter a process which can change your life.
- You can move into your imagination by physical movement. Walk, dance, cycle, jog, swim your way into new creativity. Free your mind.
- With every wish and dream you create your own reality!

28

You Can If You Think
You Can

*'Every individual forms his own
estimate of himself and that basic
estimate goes far towards determining
what he becomes. You can do no more
than you believe you can. You can be
no more than you believe you are.
Belief stimulates power within yourself.'*

NORMAN VINCENT PEALE

It has often been said that we teach what we need to learn, and I think this has been very true for me. I have always been fascinated by the concept of self-esteem (at first because I didn't have much and then because I realized that many others didn't either). In spite of all my years of research and the numerous books that I have written on and around the subject, I have to say that my own self-esteem can still be evasive and elusive; it can be as slippery as a snake and is sometimes able to disappear just as swiftly, without trace.

Our personal levels of self-esteem depend entirely on the power of our self-belief, and so everyone has self-esteem issues

because we are all always working towards greater self-awareness. It's helpful to remember this on a day when your
confidence is low, the rest of the universe looks totally together
and you feel such a mess. When our self-esteem is about to
drop through the floor we start comparison shopping. You will
recognize this condition; it develops as soon as you begin to
compare yourself (unfavourably) with everyone else and
inevitably discover that you do not come up to scratch.

High and low self-esteem

We bring our whole self to every one of our experiences. This
means that we integrate our mind, body, spirit and emotions.
Our thoughts, feelings and behaviour are interrelated; they
affect each other and create each other. And the quality of our
experiences depends upon the type of thoughts and feelings we
have and the ways in which we behave. Figure 8 shows the different thoughts, feelings and behaviour, which together create
the experiences of high and low self-esteem.

Notice how the nature of our thoughts affects our feelings and
our subsequent behaviour. The interdependency of these three
aspects means that if we can consciously change any one of the
three, then we can transform our experiences.

	High self-esteem	**Low self-esteem**
Thinks	I believe in myself.	I don't believe in myself.
	I trust my intuition.	I have no self-respect.
	I deserve the best.	I am not deserving.
	I am worthy.	I am a victim.
	I respect myself.	I am powerless.
	I respect others.	I am a failure.
	I can make things happen.	I am no good.
	I can change.	I can't change.
	I am a success.	I am too ...
	I do the best I can.	I am not good enough.
Feels	I am spontaneous.	I am uptight.
	I am free.	I am insecure.
	I am caring.	I am antisocial.
	I am optimistic.	I am depressed.
	I am appreciative.	I am guilty.
	I am balanced.	I am worried.
	I am positive.	I am critical.
	I am in touch with my emotions.	I am afraid of my emotions.
	I am secure.	I am victimized.
Behaves	I act decisively.	I act indecisively.
	I act effectively.	I act fearfully.
	I act trustingly.	I act critically.
	I act creatively.	I act judgementally.
	I act openly.	I act defensively.
	I act assertively.	I act passively/aggressively.
	I can take risks.	I can't take risks.
	I can say no.	I can't say no.
	I can show my feelings.	I can't show my feelings.
	I have good communication skills.	I have poor communication skills.

Figure 8: High and Low Self-esteem (taken from my book,
The Self-Esteem Workbook)

EXERCISE:

Maintaining your self-esteem

Think back to a time when your self-esteem suddenly plummeted;
you may have felt embarrassed or criticized or ashamed. One
minute you were fine and then suddenly you were in little pieces.
Describe how you were before the demoralizing event.

• What were your thoughts about yourself?

• How did you feel?

• How did you act?

And now answer the same questions for after the event. How did
your self-belief, feelings and behaviour change?
Reflect on the incident, thoughts, feelings and actions that cost you
your self-esteem. This process was not inevitable; how could you
have thought, felt or behaved differently? Which reactions could
you have changed? Would you have felt as deflated if you had
been able to keep believing in yourself, whatever the
circumstances? What if you could have experienced a different
emotional response? For example, if you had been able to feel
more spontaneous and optimistic you might have found a creative
way to lighten the situation. And could you have acted differently?
Maybe you didn't say what you wanted to say or perhaps you
said too much? Look for a pattern in your responses. Do you
always react to uncertainty and doubt in the same way? Once you
recognize your mental, emotional and behavioural patterns, you
are well on the way to breaking a self-induced cycle of low self-
esteem.

Self-affirmations and going through the wrong doors

When self-doubt and insecurity are eating away at your self-belief, you need to look at two things:

1. What are your personal self-affirmations?

2. Are you going through the wrong doors?

Your self-affirmations are your deeply held beliefs about yourself: I am amazing/talented/creative/caring ... Or and much more likely: I am too stupid/too lazy/not good enough ... etc. Negative self-beliefs lead us on to that self-critical path heading straight for low self-esteem. Root out your self-criticisms and start thinking and saying positively affirming statements about yourself (if you tell everyone that you are no good they will soon start to believe you). Begin to believe in yourself and demonstrate those beliefs. Show that you are confident in your own abilities and others will soon reflect your positivity.

Have you ever tormented yourself with such unanswerable questions as:

- Why do I always get the bad luck?
- How come I'm such a loser?
- Why can't someone give me a break?
- When will my life start to take off?
- Why do I always have such lousy relationships?

Such questions lead to the pain of helplessness, frustration and low self-esteem. Is there a question like this that you keep asking yourself over and over again, a question that tortures you endlessly and doesn't seem to have an answer? Think of such a question as a wrong door. I imagine a pantomime set with two doors. One has the guy with the custard pie standing behind it: this one is the wrong door! The audience is hysterical as the comic turn gets a pie in his face yet again! Exactly how many custard pies in the face does he need before he stops going through that door? And exactly how many times do you need to ask yourself self-defeating and unproductive questions before you stop and realize that this is a wrong door for you?

When you next find yourself looking low self-esteem in the eye, just remember that you can always change your responses; you don't have to go down that well-worn path of negativity. Our habitual patterns have been learned and they can be unlearned. Get out of the self-blame game and stop punishing yourself. Let yourself off these self-defeating hooks and nurture your positive self-belief. You can do this; you only need to think you can!

Reflections

- Everyone has self-esteem issues, because we are all always working towards greater self-awareness.
- When our self-esteem is about to drop through the floor, we start comparison shopping.
- Do you always react to uncertainty and doubt in the same way? Look for a pattern in your responses.
- When self-doubt and insecurity are eating away at your self-belief you need to look at two things: what are your personal self-affirmations and are you going through the wrong doors?
- Begin to believe in yourself and demonstrate those beliefs. Show that you are confident in your own abilities and others will soon reflect your positivity.
- Nurture your positive self-belief. You can do this; you only need to think you can.

29

Stop Relationship Disasters

'Relationships are mirrors of ourselves. What we attract always mirrors either qualities we have or beliefs we have about relationships.'

LOUISE HAY

Are you stuck in a relationship crisis yet again? Has he let you down, been an idiot, behaved badly? Has she had another emotional outburst and left you feeling exhausted and confused? Is this relationship worth all the hassle? If your intimate relationship is an emotional roller-coaster ride, maybe it's time to reassess the situation.

Most of us spend more time washing our hair than we do concentrating on nurturing our relationships. That fabulous excitement at the beginning of a new relationship is bound to fade as you become a regular item. And if and when you move in together and become embroiled in domestic arrangements, you will need more than a TV dinner and a glass of Chardonnay to keep the romance alive.

If you find yourself locked in argument with your partner (yet again) you need to check out the following exercise.

Why are you arguing?

Ask yourself the following questions.

1. Do you feel as if you are going over and over the same old issue? In other words, do you recognize a pattern here? If so, what is at the root of this pattern?

2. Are you feeling victimized, criticized or abused in some way? Is your partner really treating you badly or are you feeling super-sensitive and vulnerable? Again, have you had this feeling before? Is there a pattern in your reaction?

3. Are you blaming each other rather than looking for a solution to your disagreements? If so, you are in a negative cycle that only leads to more anger and resentment.

4. Do you want to make this relationship work? Is it worth the effort?

5. Do you like the ups and downs of a yo-yo relationship (making up is just so sweet)?

Yo-yo relationships

If your love life is a soap opera of rowing and making up, you might just like it like this. Some people can't resist the tension and adrenaline of an on/off relationship (never boring, ever dynamic and full of drama). If you are in a long-term yo-yo relationship, it obviously satisfies both your needs. There are a number of reasons why you may be drawn to such a turbulent love life.

Commitment-phobics (who want security but without the dreaded obligation) will be attracted to on/off relationships. Those who fear true intimacy (i.e. personal disclosure and emotional commitment) will also like yo-yoing. But both these character traits are probably only disguising deeper issues such as lack of personal inner strength and low self-worth. If one partner is very low in self-esteem they may believe that they don't deserve a stable relationship and so they play along with the other partner and become a victim of insecurity.

But when one partner outgrows the rapturous extremes and the insecurity of the emotional peaks and troughs, this sort of relationship will no longer work.

Relationship maintenance

Even if your relationship does not fall into the volatile yo-yo category, it may well need some maintenance work. Let's face it, relationships do need working on. It's short-sighted to pretend that our love lives will just sort themselves out; we create our relationships and we need to put in some effort here (before it all goes downhill fast). You want appreciation and attention and care from your partner *and your partner wants the same from you*! You get back what you give in life, and this is never so obviously true as in your intimate partnerships. If this relationship is worth it, then give it the time and attention it deserves. Don't wait until your differences are irreconcilable.

Go back to the previous exercise. Are you both caught in a cycle of blame? If this is the case then this cycle must be broken, otherwise you will stay in stalemate. The only way to break this pattern is for you each to be able to see things from the other's perspective. This is not always easy (you may both feel irritated and hard done by), but take the time to really listen to each other's viewpoint. Do not interrupt each other, listen well and try to understand. Sometimes the desire to understand each other can facilitate a breakthrough (he cares enough to try, she cares enough to listen). Agreeing to disagree may resolve the situation. Try to respect and embrace each other's differences; after all, these are what attracted you to each other in the first place.

If you recognize a repeating pattern in your disagreements you need to root it out and give it a name so that you can talk to each other about it. We often argue about trivia when we are feeling undervalued and unappreciated. It's possible that the only real problem is that you are not giving each other enough of the care and nurturing that you both need. Remember how you were at the beginning of your relationship. What were the little intimate details that glued you together? Resurrect them now! Why did you ever give them up when they were so much fun?

And if the matter is more serious and there are some deep issues to resolve, why not try some counselling support? Some people find this prospect very daunting, but ask yourself this question: 'Is this relationship worth saving?' If the answer is yes, then why not take advantage of professional help?

Your relationship is a mirror

It's important to remember that you attract the type of relationship you think you deserve. If you act like a victim you will attract a bully (your energies will be magnetic to each other). This is why so many women who have been abused by a man and managed to get away go on to have relationships with other abusers. Such a cycle can only be broken when the woman believes that she deserves a relationship that is supportive.

We are highly influenced by our parents' relationship with us and with each other. For example, if your parents were over-demanding of you when you were small, you may still be creating relationships with people who ask too much of you; if your parents were emotionally close and supportive, you are more likely to recreate such a relationship for yourself.

Our intimate relationships are always a reflection of our inner needs and expectations. If our parents had damaging relationship patterns we may still be trying to work them out in our own relationships. There is nothing unusual about this; in fact, we are all a product of our patterns. The trick is to recognize where we are stuck and how we can change. And the key to change in relationships is the knowledge that *it all begins with you*. You can never change anyone; you can only change yourself. As you learn to love and respect yourself, you will attract loving and respectful relationships. All your relationships are a reflection of the one that you have with yourself, and as you learn to be your true self, your relationships will become more harmonious, loving and supportive.

Reflections

- Most of us spend more time washing our hair than we do nurturing our relationships.
- It's short-sighted to pretend that our love lives will just sort themselves out.
- Agreeing to disagree may let you both off the hook.
- We often argue about trivia when we are feeling undervalued and unappreciated.
- You attract the type of relationship that you think you deserve.
- All your relationships are a reflection of the one you have with yourself.

30

Intuition, Your Sixth Sense

'Whether we call them hunches, gut
feelings, senses or dreams, they're all
the same thing – intuition, speaking
to us, giving us insight and knowledge
to help us make sound decisions about
any number of actions we take.
Intuition occurs when we directly
perceive facts outside the range of the
usual five senses and independently
of any reasoning process.'

MONA LISA SCHULZ

Mona Lisa Schulz MD PhD is a neuropsychiatrist and a scientist
with an extensive background in clinical medicine and brain
research. She also practises as a medical intuitive and teaches
health-care professionals how to acknowledge, trust and
develop their intuitive skills. Dr Schulz gives intuitive consulta-
tions over the phone. Someone calls and tells her their name
and age and without any other information she performs what

she calls a long distance 'reading' in which she is able to identify the person's physical condition and emotional state and can explain how the two are linked together. A well-respected academic, Dr Shultz says, 'I have always been intuitive, but I haven't always wanted to be.' In her incredible book, *Awakening Intuition: Using Your Mind–Body Network for Insight and Healing*, she describes the penalties she paid for her amazing gift as a young child. When she was seven her parents took her for a psychological evaluation because they were concerned that she wasn't normal. Although the assessment showed that she was indeed 'normal', young Mona Lisa picked up an important message, which is one that she says that most of us will have received early on in childhood, and that was that, 'intuition was bad, while intelligence was good. Intuition is suspected; intelligence is accepted.' Her book is an absolutely fascinating scientific study of the links between our mind, bodies, emotions and spirit. Above all, she demonstrates quite clearly that intuition is not a mystical talent owned by the sensitive few but a natural sixth sense that we can all use to improve the quality of our lives.

Our spiritual energy speaks to us through this instinctive gift of intuition; we *all* have intuitive powers. How many times have you looked back at a situation that has gone badly and thought, *I knew that would happen; I sensed that I should have done this, that or the other; I should have listened to my intuition.*

Women are much more likely to have experienced this than men (who usually find it harder to tap into their spiritual and emotional energy). When women access their true intuitive natures their power is formidable, and fully-grown men have been known to run in the face of this amazing 'knowingness'. You recognize that feeling, don't you, when you just *know* something is true. 'But how do you know? There's no logic to this,' most men will ask. No, and that's exactly the point; intuition taps into our deepest, instinctive awareness and there is no logical reason, but still we just *know*.

Long ago the word 'witch' was used to describe young and old women healers. One derivation for the word 'witch' is from 'wit', which means wise. The fear of the wise woman's spiritual powers led to the misuse of the term witch, so that she became a corrupt and evil power in people's minds and eventually in children's books. And so, at some level, our childhood fear of the wicked old witch in Hansel and Gretel may be provoked by an irrational fear of our own intuitive powers.

Trusting your intuition

Do you trust your intuition? Do you know where to look for it?

One of the greatest gifts we can give our children is the awareness that they can 'look inside themselves' to solve their own problems. How many of us were encouraged to do this? Were you ever told to listen and act on your 'gut' reaction or were you always taught to reason things out?

Remember that the inner voice of our intuition acts as a bridge between the physical and spiritual realms and we need to experience ourselves mentally, physically, emotionally and spiritually in order to feel centred, calm and confident. We need to balance our intellect with our intuition. Intuition is not logical, nor is it reasonable, and it is certainly not predictable. You tapped into your intuition when you had that hunch about something, when you abandoned a project and took off in a whole new direction just because it 'felt right', when you were just thinking about someone and then they phoned or you bumped into them in the street. Most of us have heard our inner voice, but we are often afraid to act on it. If an action appears to be irrational it's hard to explain our reasons to others, and as soon as we start to try to explain (rationalize) our intuitive feelings, they lose their power. We need to learn to *trust* and then to *act* upon our intuitive voice.

EXERCISE:

You and your intuition

Sit quietly in a comfortable position and take some deep breaths. Relax your body and your mind and focus your thoughts on your intuition.

What feelings do you associate with your intuition? Are these feelings pleasant or frightening (or anything else)?

Think of three times that you have followed your intuition and things have turned out well.

1. . . . .

2. . . . .

3. . . . .

Now, think of three things that your intuitive voice has been urging you to do. These can be small things (reply to a letter, contact a friend) or they may be larger matters (change a job, walk away from a relationship).

1. . . . .

2. . . . .

3.

Why haven't you acted on the advice of your intuition?

Intuition is one of the voices of our Higher Self and it speaks to us through urges, dreams, feelings, symbols and flashes of insight. To hear our intuition we need to listen to our inner world of thoughts, feelings and senses. Intuition always draws us to the things that give us energy and feed our creativity. When we trust that inner voice we are true to ourselves and others; we are real and genuine in our communications and we are willing to try new things because they feel right.

What sort of future do you want for yourself? Would you like to do something totally different? You may wish to make a change in your life but find that you keep creating excuses to stop you putting your plans into action. Maybe you are afraid to follow your intuition because it involves stepping into the unknown and taking a risk. If you deny the voice of your intuition you will never feel fulfilled, happy and peaceful; you will always be looking for something more.

EXERCISE:

Listening to that inner voice

Our lives just whizz by, don't they? Who has the time or inclination to make intuitive connections? But we must make time and find a space in our busy schedule to allow our intuitive thoughts to flow.

Take some time every day, even if it's only a few minutes, to tune into your intuition. Find a quiet spot where you won't be interrupted, close your eyes and relax your body. Breathe deeply and slowly and relax your mind. If your thoughts intrude, just let them go and bring your concentration back to your breathing. In this relaxed and quiet state you can allow your intuition to come through. Be prepared to 'hear' it in any number of different ways. Some people recognize their voice and others don't have any immediate awareness. You may experience strong feelings or you may not. One of the best ways to make your connection is to ask your intuition for guidance on a particular matter. Make your question as specific as possible and then let go of all preconceived ideas about how your answer will come. Give yourself some quiet time so that your intuition can focus on your dilemma. Then, when you have finished, let go of all thoughts about this matter. Your inner guidance can come at any time and in any shape or form – the words of a song, a book open at a certain page, a chance meeting, a strong feeling that you should act in a certain way – so let your mind stay open to all possibilities. When you hear the message of your inner voice, you will just *know* what to do. And then all you have to do is DO IT!

Reflections

- Intuition is one of the voices of your Higher Self. Listen carefully to make your spiritual connection.
- We have not been encouraged to develop our inner wisdom and we may even feel afraid of unleashing this power. Don't be afraid. Trust your intuition; there is so much to gain.
- To feel centred, calm and confident you need to balance your intellect with your intuition.
- Ask yourself why you sometimes ignore the messages that your intuition is sending you.
- Tune in to your intuition regularly and let your mind stay open to all possibilities; inner guidance can come anywhere, at any time in any way.
- When you hear the message of your inner voice you will just *know* what to do. Do it.

31

Are You Stuck
in a Rut?

*'Remember that you become what you
practise most.'*

RICHARD CARLSON

Has your life lost its zing? Are you feeling jaded and uninspired?
Don't just sit in your boredom and slip even lower into the
depths of negativity. Recognize that whenever you feel stuck
and fed up it's time for a change; you have outgrown your old
perceptions and you are ready for something new.

Time can slip by almost unnoticed as we get up each day and
do whatever it is we do. But if we aren't paying attention to the
details of our life then we are missing the whole point. Think
through a typical day, being aware of all the things that you
always do. This list will probably include such items as the time
you get up, what you have for breakfast, your teeth cleaning
and showering habits, the route you take to work, the contents
of your shopping trolley, what you like for lunch and so on.

Whenever you lose your enthusiasm for life you can be sure
that you have become a victim of your own habits. Of course
we need some structures and repetition to keep ourselves
together, but what price are you paying for your togetherness?
Are you suffocating your natural spontaneity and creativity by

sticking to too many personal rules and habitual responses? Are you stuck in a rut (or several ruts)? Are you losing your buzz?

Living on autopilot

You have most likely had the experience of driving to a familiar destination and arriving with no memory of the journey. Well, a life full of well-practised routines and reactions can also be run on autopilot. But life isn't a dress rehearsal for the real thing – *it is the real thing!* Boredom and apathy are indicators of a need for increased self-awareness and reflection.

Some of our daily habits are fairly obvious and can be changed quite easily (go for a different haircut, try a new recipe, take an alternative route to work). But such simple external changes will not be enough to recharge our batteries and inject us with the fascination and enthusiasm that we are seeking. For real, positive life-changing change we need to look closely at our deep-seated mental, emotional and behavioural patterns.

Looking at your life

Take a good long look at your life; be totally aware of this moment. What are you feeling and thinking? Are you conscious of what is going on or are you acting out of habit? Open your heart and mind to the details of your life. Pay attention to your decision-making process. Are you fulfilling your own needs or just fitting in with what others want?

And what do you want? Are you living life your way or are you putting your dreams on hold for some reason? What do you expect from others and what do you get? Do you smile a lot or are you sad? Allow yourself to look at what is really going on. Put your life under a magnifying glass; what important details have you been missing? What have you discovered?

Now tell the truth to yourself. What are the patterns that are holding you back? What do you believe about yourself? Perhaps you don't believe that you deserve to get what you want. Are you able to express your feelings or are you afraid to? Do you ever let people use you as a doormat? Why are you putting up with less than the best?

EXERCISE:

Deciding to change

Think of a situation that you are finding hard to handle.

1. Describe the problem.

2. What exactly would you like to change?

3. Describe your ideal situation (in as much detail as possible).

4. What part did you play in helping to create this difficult situation? Look objectively at your behaviour. Have you been honest about your feelings? Have you been clear about where you stand?

5. What is the first step you would need to take to start changing the present situation?

6. What attitudes or beliefs would you need to change in order to take this first step? In other words, what are the negative patterns that have helped to create the original problem?

Everything's coming up roses

But only if you've planted them! Our habitual patterns have grown from our beliefs. For example, if I believe in myself I will have an optimistic outlook that will attract more of the same, whereas if I believe that life's a bitch, then this will be my experience. We get what we expect to get. And if we keep on doing the same thing we will get the same results. Are you getting the results you desire? Are others treating you with respect? Do you keep getting locked in the same old arguments? Do you love what you do or is it just a chore? Are you living in a rose garden or in a mess of weeds?

Change is easy; it all begins with you. Your habits are only learned behaviours; they are not set in stone (although this may sometimes feel very hard to believe). We become what we practise most, so watch what you are practising. Replace the habits that don't work for you with ones that do; create new, positive life-affirming patterns that support your development and growth. Accept responsibility for the quality of your life and focus on what you want rather than what you don't want. Believe in yourself and your capacity to change and know that you can break all your inhibiting habits and patterns. As you reach beyond your old limitations you will feel a remarkable increase in your energy and confidence. Life will become more interesting and expansive, and you will be buzzing again.

Reflections

- If your life has lost its zing, it's time for a change.
- If you lose your enthusiasm you can be sure that you have become a victim of your own habits.
- Boredom and apathy are indicators of a need for increased self-awareness and reflection.
- For life-changing change we need to look closely at our deep-seated patterns.
- We become what we practise most, so watch what you are practising.
- Open your heart and mind to the details of your life.

32

Don't Become a
Self-help Junkie

*'Why not today? Forget yesterday, and
all the other yesterdays. Let them fade
away. TODAY is the time to begin and
NOW is the moment.'*

KENNETH THURSTON HURST

Yesterday is gone and tomorrow never comes. The point of
power is always in the present moment. *Carpe Diem* (seize the
day) and decide to go for what you want, *right now*. Change
brings magic into our lives but the potential for excitement is
often outweighed by our fears and inhibitions. You can read
every self-help book in the universe and still not be able to
change your life; you can attend personal development workshops and still feel stuck; you can meditate to clear your mind
and still not be able to clear up your problems. It's quite
possible to become a self-help junkie: addicted to the *idea* of
change and still looking for answers in the outer world (books,
teachers, gurus, counsellors, therapies).

In times of difficulty we all seek opinions, validation,
guidance and support from others; this is how we gather infor-

176 | BE YOURSELF

mation, look for new directions and begin making life-changing decisions. But our search can actually become an end in itself. If you have a shelf-full of self-help books and *still* feel that you can't help yourself, maybe it's time to begin, right now!

There are so many ways that we can give our power away and some of these ways are quite subtle and hard to detect. Let's go back to the example of the self-help junkie. How ironic that in the very quest for personal power we may be just giving it away. This can happen if we think that intellectual awareness is the same thing as self-awareness. There is a huge chasm between knowledge and experience. If you read all the tips in this book but never used any of them, they could never work for you. Or you can give power away by attributing your counsellor/ friend/parent with more power to understand you than you have yourself. This can never be the true state of affairs; no one but *you* can know the real you. While wise guidance is helpful, it is only valuable in so far as you can resonate with its meaning and take appropriate action on your own behalf. No one can think, believe, feel or act for you. Your life is your own, make of it what you will.

Just for today

At the centre of yourself is a place where you:

- Feel self-respect and self-worth
- Can make decisions
- Have high energy and are focused on the present
- Are imaginative and creative
- Can take responsibility for all your actions
- Feel trusting towards yourself and the rest of the universe

- Are not afraid to take chances
- Know that you have your own power
- Are ready to get a grip on your life

Imagine this place where you can take charge of your own destiny and really be yourself. Now step into the centre of this place. Feel your power, optimism and energy and know that the world is your oyster. Suspend your disbeliefs (you can pick them all up again tomorrow!) and just for today choose to live your life your way. What would you love to do? Take the first step now. There are no let-outs today, no ifs or buts or maybes. Excuses won't wash – you can only be true to yourself. Things will need to be said and done; changes are ahead. Go forward and embrace them.

Have you taken your first step or are you still reading all these words? This book won't change your life, only you can do that. You can only experience feeling at the very centre of your life if you are prepared to face your fears, take some risks and act! Don't give your power away to someone you think might know you better than you know yourself. If you are still dithering, try the next exercise.

Helping yourself

The self-help industry is ever expanding and offers all sorts of brilliant resources but it only provides the tools you need; you have to do the work yourself. I have a vast array of self-help material which inspires and encourages me, but that's all it can do. Affirmations and visualizations can't work if you don't do them. Positive thinking techniques need application. Forgiveness will free up your energy, but you have to do the work (and forgiving does take some doing). It's not enough to know that you are running on negative patterns; you need to find out what these are and then change them. Self-help requires that you do just that. Help yourself to move forwards. You have all the power, energy and grace that you need. Your true self is only waiting to be discovered.

EXERCISE:

As good and as bad as it can be

1. Specify three things that you long to do but are afraid to try.

a. . . . .

b. . . . .

c. . . . .

2. What do you think would be the best and the worst possible outcomes of doing each of these three things?

Best possible outcome   **Worst possible outcome**

a. . . . .

b. . . . .

c. . . . .

3. Ask yourself, 'What are my fears and anxieties?' and write them down.

4. Now ask yourself, 'How realistic are my fears and anxieties?'

Rate your score for realism on a scale of 1–10 (1 = totally unrealistic, 10 = totally realistic).
How realistic are your fears? Usually our fears are irrational and groundless and our longing by far outweighs the reality of the fear. Go ahead and just do whatever needs to be done. You will feel fabulous.

Reflections

- Today is the time to begin, and now is the moment!
- It's quite possible to become addicted to the *idea* of inner change while always looking for answers in the outside world.
- No one but *you* can know the real you.
- Step into the centre of your life and experience your power.
- How realistic are your fears?
- Self-help requires that you do just that – help yourself.

33

Meditating in the Supermarket, on the Bus, in the Shower and Everywhere

'Meditation is a bridge between the inner and outer self; the physical, mental, emotional, spiritual self. The more connections you make between your inner and outer world the more integrated you will become.'

GREER ALLICA

Many years ago when I was going through a difficult time I suddenly found that nothing 'out there' in the world could make me feel better: not my faithful friends, my beautiful children, my health, my family, my creative efforts – nothing was enough. I felt disenchanted by life's goodies and that was a lonely and depressing feeling. In desperation I started to read about spiritual practices and meditation, and a new and fantastic world began to open before my eyes. The Chinese word for 'crisis' is the same as the word for 'opportunity' and it is true that when one door closes many others open (if we keep looking for them).

Although I knew that meditation would put me in touch with my inner self, I found it hard to discipline myself to periods of silent contemplation. But I really needed something that would give me a link with the spiritual while I was buzzing about doing worldly things with my young children. And then I came across an amazing technique, a true example of practical spirituality, that opens the door to a meditative state, *wherever you are* and *whatever you are doing*. This mind-expanding and easy-to-use technique was created by the Russian philosopher-mystic, George Gurdjieff. He called the process 'self-remembering' and introduced the concept of the 'witness'. But before we consider this technique we need to look at who you think you really are.

Who do you think you are?

How many 'yous' are there inside you? Not such a silly question when you think about how many emotions you have felt today. For example, since this morning I have been focused, irritated, hungry, chatty, creative, tired, reflective, happy, solemn, active ... and these are just the feelings that I can remember. We play so many parts throughout our day and who 'you' are changes at every moment (see Figure 9). However, as we know, there is much more to us than a variety of emotional states: our Higher Self transcends our earthly links. So how can we rise above the numerous roles that we play from day to day; how can seek our divine connection when we are all tied up in our desires, feelings and thoughts?

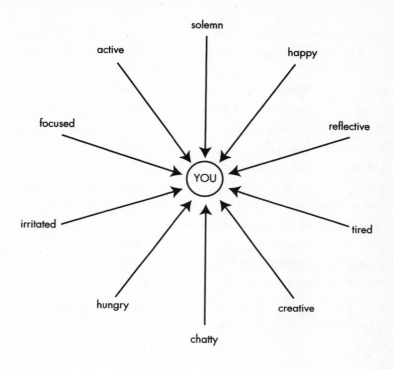

Figure 9: How Many 'Yous' Are There Inside You?

Make a diagram for yourself like Figure 9 above. Reflect upon all the 'yous' that you have been today. Now take each one and think about how you identify with that transitory state at this moment. Is it very important now? Can you even remember the moods of this morning? Each of these 'yous' represents an identification with a worldly thought or emotion. The way to transcend this condition and to make our spiritual connection is to recognize and to break these identifications. When we reflect upon our numerous 'yous' it becomes possible to devalue their importance: we can often let ourselves off the hook by lessening the power that we give to these transitory 'you' states.

Gurdjieff points out that sometimes one 'you' does something for which every other 'you' must pay, perhaps for the rest of your life. Have you ever done something for which you can't forgive yourself? Perhaps you said the wrong thing or treated someone badly and are still carrying remorse and feelings of guilt. The 'you' who made this mistake is just one of your many faces: your 'yous' are numerous and ephemeral, and all are judgmental. Sometimes we can let one 'you' ruin our lives; let's get this in perspective and give ourselves a break. We are so much more than we think we are. Self-remembering and the witness demonstrates this beautifully.

How to meditate here, there and everywhere

Ramakrishna tells us that the emancipated soul 'lives in the world like a diver bird. It dives into water, but the water does not wet its plumage'. The following technique helps us to be like this diver bird: it shows us that it is possible to be in the world and still maintain a stable, spiritual centre.

When you use self-remembering you adopt the role of witness as you go about your daily affairs. The witness observes all that you do but is non-evaluative and doesn't judge your actions. For example, you might eat a chocolate bar (an act of desire) and then get annoyed with yourself for having eaten it. The witness (when it arrives) would note:

1. She is eating a chocolate bar.
2. She is annoyed with herself for eating a chocolate bar.

The witness is dispassionate and does not care what you do; it only makes a note of what you do (it is never emotionally involved). It takes concentration to remain in the witness state, and when you begin to use this technique you will often find yourself forgetting to witness (getting emotionally involved) and then suddenly later (maybe hours or even days later) remembering to witness again. The following description of witnessing, taken from the brilliant book *Be Here Now* by Ram Dass, describes this dilemma perfectly:

> You are walking down a street witnessing yourself walking down a street. You feel happy and witness feeling happy ... and so it goes on. Then you meet someone or see something that irritates you. Immediately you get irritated and forget all about the witness. The adrenaline pumps through you and you think angry thoughts. At this point 'angry me' is who you are. Only *much* later do you remember that you were attempting to witness.
>
> At that point you promise yourself that you won't forget again. Ah, how little you know about the subtleties of the seductions of the other 'yous'. Again you are walking and again witnessing walking and so forth. This time you meet with another situation which irritates you. Again you lose your witness (or centre as it is sometimes called) and again your endocrine glands secrete and you think angry thoughts. But this time right in the middle of the entire drama you 'wake up' ... That is, you realize your predicament. But at this point it is difficult to get free of 'angry you' because you are already getting much gratification. (It's a bit like trying to stop in the midst of a sexual act.)

Witnessing

1. Start witnessing now. Put down the book and wander about a bit observing (witnessing) your actions. Don't think too much about it; just imagine stepping outside of yourself and watching your thoughts, feelings and actions. At first it may help to talk your way through it. For example: I am walking to the back door; I'm opening the door and going down the garden path; I am enjoying looking at the flowers; I can see a lot of weeds; I feel thirsty; I'm going back to the kitchen; I'm making a cup of tea; I'm feeling tired ... Sounds easy? Try it and see how long you can last. See if you can concentrate for as long as 10 minutes.

What happened? Was it easy or hard? At what point (if any) did you forget to witness? Was it a strange sensation? Did you enjoy it?

2. Now go out into the world and practise. Try it anywhere and everywhere and don't tell anyone what you are doing. The more you do it, the easier it will become. I love to practise witnessing in a busy supermarket – it just changes the whole experience.

At first you may find that witnessing is easier to stick at when you are not feeling particularly emotionally involved in what's happening. Start to notice the trigger points where you forget to observe because you have become emotionally 'hooked' into an experience. (In our example I might see the weeds, get cross with them and so lose the witness state.) Use this technique as often as you can remember. The more you do, the more powerful it will become. When you take the witness role you begin to create a calm centre within yourself. This centre is a place where you can learn to break your identification with your transitory 'you' states and so rise above your material and emotional attachments. When you can transcend your desires in this way you can experience the true nature of your spirituality.

Witnessing is easy, fun and changes the way you see the world. Don't be too serious about it and don't get annoyed with yourself when you suddenly 'wake up' to remember you were supposed to be witnessing and lost focus hours ago. The important thing to notice when you do forget is what took you off course. What emotional state took you on a detour? Witnessing creates concentration, focus and self-awareness, and these together create a portal to the meditative state. Go through that portal and you will find it easier and easier to experience being alone with yourself in silence, a skill that opens the door to the invisible spiritual world.

Reflections

- Meditation acts like a bridge to link your inner and outer self.
- We can only make our true spiritual connection when we can break with worldly emotional attachments: our Higher Self transcends our earthly links.
- The beliefs or actions of one (fleeting) 'you' state can ruin your life. Remember that you are so much more than any one of your 'you' states.
- Spiritual freedom lies in our ability to be *of* the world rather than *in* the world; live your life like a diver bird.
- The calm centre of the witness state allows you to experience your divine connection with your Higher Self; cultivate this centre.
- Focus, concentration and self-awareness are skills that open the portal to the invisible world of the spirit.

34

When You Just Don't Like Yourself Very Much

'The curious paradox is that when I accept myself just as I am, then I can change.'

When we discover that we play an active part in creating the circumstances of our life, it feels like such a revelation. Up until this time we might have been under the illusion that whatever happened to us was all in the lap of the gods, that we were at the mercy of the fates, that life and people were busy doing things to us and that we could only take a passive role. Yes, when we know that we can choose not to be a victim, we take responsibility for ourselves and our actions, and we embark upon a fascinating path of creativity and self-change.

This path of personal development has its ups and downs: there are times when we can feel so clear and centred, only to be followed by times when we feel yet more confusion and doubt. There is a temptation to believe that we are moving towards a finite point of awareness and that when we 'get there'

188 | BE YOURSELF

we will at last understand the true meaning and purpose of our life. But this path has many twists and turns and diversions, and there is no 'end' to it while we are still alive. Our awareness grows in fits and starts. We are a work in progress, ever moving, ever changing and always evolving.

Good guy/bad guy

When life is sweet, so are we. It's so easy to feel good about ourselves when we are being kind, thoughtful, caring and generous. When we are radiating positive energy we are high in self-esteem and we are demonstrating our highest qualities. We are in touch with our real and true self (balanced, centred and whole). However, we always need to recognize that we are ordinary human beings with our own weaknesses and frailties. As we become more self-aware and start to use techniques and strategies to enhance our lives, we can easily fall into a subtle trap of our own making.

We can measure our self-improvement in any number of ways, including levels of self-esteem, feelings of openness, awareness of the needs of others, ability to use good communication skills and increased feelings of peace and calm. We may just begin to feel that we are becoming a 'better' person (and indeed we are probably making many positive changes) when, out of the blue, we find ourselves having nasty thoughts or not behaving very well. And then we feel disappointed, lose our self-respect and *we don't like ourselves any more*. Self-criticism and self-dislike take us right back into the negativity that we have been trying so hard to leave behind. So, what's to be done?

Let's go back to the idea that each human being is a work in progress (never static, ever developing and changing). We evolve and progress by facing and overcoming our challenges, and life will never fail to provide them for us! There are many aspects to the self; one of them we could call our 'small' self. We all have a 'small' self; (s)he's the guy who suddenly gets afraid of all this openness and trust and wants to back off into a tight corner and protect her/his interests. When we retreat into our 'small' self we become defensive, close down and lose faith in our self and in others.

Imagine a situation where a close relationship has reached a new level of intimacy. The two of you have been getting closer and revealing more about yourselves to each other and the energy is good between you. And then something happens (you feel criticized, threatened or just plain scared); it all becomes too much and you withdraw into your 'small' self. The former feelings of closeness and connection are then replaced with a sense of being separate and feeling alone and victimized.

So it seems that on the one hand we have a good guy (our balanced and centred self) who is positive and prepared to take risks, and on the other hand a bad guy (our 'small' self) who shrinks away into negativity and limitation when the going gets tough. But actually there is no conflict of interests here: our 'small' self is not really a baddie at all. Each time we turn away from our true self to hide in our fearful smaller version, we are actually being shown the places within us that need healing and support in order for us to develop and grow. Whenever you become less than your best, look inside yourself to find out why. What has triggered your fears? Why are you being defensive? What positive steps can you take to help yourself? The key to self-change is always self-acceptance; self-dislike will always inhibit our growth. There is no bad guy inside you; there is only someone who is striving to become the very best they can be, so let yourself off this hook! Self-appreciation is a key that opens the door to positive self-development. But how can we learn to appreciate the parts of ourselves that we least admire?

Loving ourselves just the way we are

We are creatures of many parts, and until we can accept our most 'unacceptable' thoughts, emotions and behaviours, we will never be free to fulfil our true potential. We can give ourselves such a hard time by denying our true feelings. Many years ago when I first began to explore my spirituality I was living on my own with two very small children. I so desperately wanted to be (and appear to be) calm, tranquil and 'spiritual'. Most of the time I wasn't feeling at all peaceful and centred, but I didn't appreciate that we can't always be serene and relaxed. It felt impossible to reconcile the way I wanted to be and the way I really felt. I didn't like the part of me that was tired, stretched and irritable; my vision and my reality were entirely different. How easy it is to punish ourselves when we don't realize that it's quite all right (and perfectly natural) to feel conflicting emotions. My spiritual development would certainly have been enhanced if I could have let myself off this hook of saintly perfection and just accepted my real feelings instead of beating myself up for not being 'spiritual enough'. It is only when we can love and accept ourselves *just the way we are* that we become able to make changes (it is indeed a paradox).

EXERCISE:

How I like to see myself/ don't like to see myself *

What patterns of behaviour, thoughts and feelings do you admire in yourself? What patterns do you consider less than admirable? Put a Y for 'yes' after the words that describe the ways in which you like to see yourself. Put an N for 'no' after the words that describe ways in which you don't like to see yourself.

MEAN	THOUGHTFUL	MOODY
KIND	IN DEMAND	THIN
GENEROUS	JEALOUS	HAPPY
ANGRY	RESPECTABLE	CARING
CONTROLLED	FAT	UNKIND
BORING	EMOTIONAL	ENERGETIC
SELFISH	HUMOUROUS	RESENTFUL
GIVING	BUBBLY	SAD
INTELLECTUAL	DEPRESSED	UNATTAINABLE
DULL	UPTIGHT	ABLE
ROMANTIC	SERENE	BLOATED
SNAPPY	ADDICTED	TEMPERAMENTAL
OUT OF CONTROL	PEACEFUL	OLD
SPIRITUAL	SEXUAL	VIOLENT
FRIENDLY	ATTRACTIVE	ARTICULATE
POPULAR	CULTURED	NARROW-MINDED
INCOMPETENT	CAPABLE	ACTIVE
GRACEFUL	STUPID	EMBARRASSED
EDUCATED	CLUMSY	SOPHISTICATED
HAIRY	UP-FRONT	NON-JUDGEMENTAL
REFINED	MYSTERIOUS	BIGOTED
ATTRACTIVE	WEAK	LITERARY
FLABBY	SPARKLING	SEDUCTIVE
NEEDY	WITHDRAWN	USEFUL
HEALTHY	CREATIVE	CONFIDENT
AGGRESSIVE	RELIABLE	GREEDY
IDIOTIC	ASSERTIVE	NEGATIVE
SUCCESSFUL	SOOTHING	COMPETITIVE

* Taken from my book, *Self-Esteem for Women*

1. Choose the four words with which you most like to identify – the words with the most powerful 'yes'.

2. Is it important that other people see you like this? If so, why is it important?

3. How do you feel about yourself on the days when you are not displaying these qualities?

4. Choose the four words with which you least like to identify – the words with the most powerful 'no'.

5. Why don't you like these characteristics?

6. How do you feel about yourself when you display these characteristics?

Accepting ourselves warts and all

Reflect on your answers to the exercise above. How do your personal likes and dislikes affect the ways in which you see yourself? How can you learn to accept your most unlovable characteristics?

Let's take anger as an example of a possible unacceptable emotion. We need to accept our anger when we feel it (just like any other emotion) but this is difficult because there is a strong cultural belief that anger is bad (and frightening). I'm not advocating antisocial or dangerous behaviour here; I'm not suggesting, for example, that it's OK to be angry and to express that anger in ways that hurt others. But if we deny our anger (or indeed any emotion) our feelings just go underground (ready to explode at any time). And if we hate ourselves for our anger we also fall into a deep pit of negativity. When any emotion is considered taboo it has a powerful hold over us. Far better to face up to our true feelings and then we can deal with them in a measured and appropriate way.

And, no, it's not a good day when I wake up feeling bloated, resentful and negative but want to see myself as sparkling, attractive and in control. But if I hate myself for feeling low there will be no chance of me getting out from under the duvet, let alone getting out into the world in a more upbeat frame of mind. If we can accept our unattractive patterns, then they have no power over us. So, if resentment is bringing me down it doesn't have to ruin my day; I only need to ask myself why I feel like this and then get on and do something about it. Bloated? Well, if I cut back on the carbohydrates I know I will soon feel much better. Negative? I recognize that I'm not a victim unless I choose to be, so I choose positivity instead!

Being your own best friend

When you just don't like yourself very much, become your own best friend instead of your own worst enemy. Step outside your own shoes for a moment and imagine yourself through the eyes of a loving, caring friend. What would that friend say to you? How would she encourage you? She would be forgiving and supportive and she wouldn't care how many mistakes you had made. Be your own best friend and embrace and accept all the parts of you that make you who you are; this *is* your whole self!

Reflections

- The path of personal development has its ups and downs!
- We are a work in progress, ever moving, ever changing and always evolving.
- Each time we turn away from our true self to hide in our fearful smaller version, we are actually being shown the places within us that need healing and support in order for us to develop and grow.
- Self-appreciation is a key that opens the door to positive self-development.
- It is only when we can accept ourselves *just the way we are* that we are able to make changes.
- Be your own best friend and embrace and accept all the parts of you that make you who you are. This is your whole self!

35

Are You Body Confident?

'My God, there are so many parts of my body that I don't like: my stomach, my bottom. I have body issues like every other woman. I'm insecure. I never think I'm thin enough or my breasts are big enough.'

GWYNETH PALTROW

Thus speaks the divine Ms Paltrow: heaven help the rest of us!

Why have we all got 'body issues'? What lies behind our obsession with weight, looks and shape? Why are our real body parts (love handles, double chins, childbearing hips, strong thighs and pear-shaped bottoms) considered ugly? Why do so many women with a high media profile lose about a quarter of their body weight when they hit the big time? Why on earth should fame and success contribute to huge weight losses?

The questions are endless and the answers can only be found in what seems to be an Alice in Wonderland World where everything is upside-down and nothing means what it says it does. How can we get a grip on body awareness, self-image and confidence issues when the messages we receive are so mixed and muddled? Do you share my confusion? Do you know why love handles and other flabby bits are a taboo subject when nearly everyone wobbles in at least one area of their body? The adoration of the bony bum and the fear and loathing of a less than flat stomach can trap us in a crazy, glossy world where unrealistically thin women are our role models and we can never have a body that is 'good enough'.

We don't think big is beautiful

A top magazine recently commissioned a survey about attitudes to body size. Five thousand women were interviewed, and the overall conclusion drawn from the results was that we do not think big is beautiful; in other words our size does matter. And it appears to matter a lot. It can hardly be a great revelation to us that, according to the survey, 8 out of 10 women think about their shape every day (how many times a day, I wonder?), 90 per cent do not believe that a woman who is overweight can be happy with her size, and more than 80 per cent feel inhibited by their body.

Why are women (and increasingly men) so hung up in the body department? And what can we do to extricate ourselves from this comparison game that always leaves us feeling less than our best?

It's no good going on about how we 'should' just be happy with what we are and how shallow it is to be concerned with our body image. We all want to look our best and I have met very few women who have no interest in their own weight (ask almost any woman and she will know exactly how much she weighs). We are preoccupied with our bodies because our culture adores and venerates youth, slimness and beauty. How can we not be affected by all the hype? We don't all want to be stick insects but neither do we want a flabby midriff; surely this cannot be a mind-blowing revelation?

Body confidence test

Yet another major survey demonstrates that most of us are suffering what could be called the Bridget Jones Syndrome. In other words, we lack body confidence and are constantly preoccupied with the way that we look. A staggering 90 per cent of the 5,000 women taking part in the survey said that the appearance of their body depressed them, and one in ten admitted to being on a 'constant' diet.

Answer 'yes', 'no' or 'sometimes' to the following questions and discover just how you really feel about your body.

1. Do you feel physically strong and powerful?

2. Do you hate any part of your body?

3. Would you say that you are obsessed by the food you eat/don't eat?

4. Do you feel free to enjoy eating?

5. Do you weigh yourself more than twice a week?

6. Do you think that you would be happier if you lost weight?

7. Are you ever embarrassed by your body?

8. Do you compare yourself with other women (men)?

9. Do you think that looks are more important than skills and abilities?

10. Would you like to have a positive self-image?

Isn't cellulite a type of battery?

And at last, a survey that can raise a laugh. Another piece of research by a top beauty firm has revealed that one in three men have no idea what cellulite is and one in five think it is a type of battery!

In different times our Rubenesque proportions and dimply bits would have been revered and admired, but in the 21st century cellulite is big business (with treatments and detoxifying procedures galore). And so we have been convinced that our oh-so-natural orange-peel thighs and dimply bottoms are merely a sight for sore eyes and yet another reason for us to lose confidence in ourselves. If we are sincere in our declaration that we are only trying to look good for our own sakes we can surely let go of the cellulite obsession.

Becoming body confident

Most of us have an inclination to criticize and dislike our bodies (it's an extension of the belief that we are not 'good enough' just the way we are). Ask anybody you know (the thin, the fat, the gorgeous, the plain) if they are happy with their body and they will probably give you a great list of complaints. Just try this and see.

Acknowledge and accept this tendency towards self-criticism and then decide to fight back! Sexy images surround us: everywhere we look we see gorgeous nubile young things radiating glamour and physical perfection. Recognize these airbrushed images for what they are: unreal and designed to make you feel dissatisfied so that you will go out and buy the product that will make your dreams come true! Extricate yourself from the madness of a relentless pursuit of what our society deems to be the perfect face and body (you will always fail to deliver).

A stick of mascara or even a new dress will not make you feel complete and happy; those feelings come from within.

Your body is a perfect machine but it won't run happily if you hate it. Body confidence creates an amazing aura of glamour. The most alluring person in the room is generally the one who radiates self-esteem and knows that she is so much more than her dress size.

10 tips to create a positive self-image

Body confidence is not dependent on how you look on the outside; it is all about how you feel about yourself on the inside. Try the following tips.

- Stop comparison shopping. When you compare yourself with others you will almost always feel intimidated.
- Love and appreciate all that your body does for you. You are perfect just the way you are.
- Celebrate your unique qualities and optimize your best features.
- Always be a first-rate version of yourself rather than a second-rate version of someone else.
- Look beyond the image in the mirror and see the talented and creative woman that you are.
- Enjoy the fantasy of glossy media hype but don't let impossible dreams steal your happiness.
- Use assertive body language. Walk tall and carry yourself with pride and you will feel so much better about yourself.
- Smile and the world smiles with you. Laugh more and you will look and feel great.

- Keep your energy levels high by making sure that you eat well and take enough exercise. When your energy is buzzing and positive you look and feel wonderful.
- A positive self-image attracts attention. Become an exciting and interesting person who radiates self-confidence and knows that there is much more to life than being a size 10!

EXERCISE:

Getting things in perspective

Let's remove our body parts from under the microscope of our attention and focus on something much more meaningful. For example, rather than asking 'Why have I got cellulite?' you could ask 'What is the real meaning of my life?' Put the focus of your attention where it will bring positive life-affirming results. Get things back into perspective by answering the following questions.

1. Who are the people you love most in all the world?
2. What quality do you most admire in yourself?
3. If you only had one week to live what would you say to whom?
4. What would you love to accomplish?
5. Are you afraid to take chances?
6. What values are most important to you?
7. Do you believe in yourself?
8. What is your most wonderful achievement?
9. Do you love life?
10. What holds you back?

Think about your answers over the coming weeks. When you find yourself preoccupied with minutiae (sagging body parts, a broken nail, a bad-hair day) lift yourself up and take a larger perspective. You are here to make the very best of your life by realizing your full potential. Make your contribution count and remember that the quality of your life is more important than the way you look.

Reflections

- We can easily become trapped in a crazy glossy world where we can never have a body that is 'good enough'.
- Stop comparison shopping or you will always feel intimidated.
- Love and appreciate all that your body does for you.
- A positive self-image attracts attention.
- The quality of your life is more important than the way you look.
- Make your contribution count.

36

Taking the Breath
of Life

*'Learning to breathe properly, with full
feeling, gives you the ability quite
literally to "inspire" yourself.'*

DAN MILLMAN

Career success, material comforts, physical fitness, loving family
and supportive relationships go a long way towards creating a
satisfying and happy life. However, all these rewards will fail to
deliver the long-term serenity and peace, and a sense of the true
meaning of our life until we discover the unseen world that lies
all around and within us. We look everywhere for this added
dimension, and the 'spiritual' marketplace certainly offers a vast
and sometimes bewildering supply of goods to meet the
growing demand for spiritual realization: self-help books,
personal development courses, spiritual awareness groups,
rebirthing, meditation, drumming, chanting, feng shui ...

The huge development in the 'spiritual awareness' business
surely reflects the amazing turn-around of a consumer-driven
society that is beginning to discover that the 'things' of the
world do not offer the ultimate prize, a happy and contented
heart. However, it seems that we are still trying to 'buy' our

spirituality – which book to read, which course to go on, which class to attend?

The best things in life are free

Our emotions are capable of turning our lives into a fairground ride. As we go up and down and round and round we can often feel totally out of control. But by learning to control our breathing we can lift our consciousness and find that calm centre within (however turbulent the emotional currents are around us). It surely is a splendid irony that such a profound tool for spiritual development is to be found in something that we already do every moment of every day and *there is no charge*.

How often are you aware of your breathing? Many of us are only conscious of our breath when feel as if we're 'running out' of it (bad cough/hurrying for a bus/head full of cold/polluted atmosphere).

Ask someone to take a deep breath. Watch for the following: raised shoulders, stomachs pulled in, chests protruding, noisy gasps. Try it yourself.

Become aware of your breathing patterns for the rest of the day and, although this may be difficult (we breathe so automatically), take note of variations and changes. Does your breathing stop and start? Do you ever hold your breath (often accompanied by putting a hand over the mouth)? Whenever you feel tension in your chest, this means that you can only breathe in shallow gulps, which then leads to more tension in your upper body.

Now sit comfortably with your back straight and, just for a few moments, raise your shoulders and breathe with shallow breaths using your upper chest rather than your abdomen. Now you know why this is called 'tension breathing'. This is how we breathe when we are uptight (a good description of the state of our upper body), and doesn't it feel exhausting and nerve-wracking? Just *not* the thing to do when feeling tense. When you have recovered and are breathing normally, check how many times you breathe in a minute. Do this now before you read on.

Most people take 12–18 breaths per minute, which is incredible when you consider this amazing fact: *when we breathe eight breaths a minute or less, our entire metabolism changes and we become relaxed, confident and capable. We are perceived as authoritative and charismatic, and we feel it!* Why weren't we taught to breathe in this way? Actually, we have always known how to breathe like this; watch a baby breathing naturally from deep in her body with relaxed and balanced in and out breaths. Then she grows up to face the emotional, mental and physical strains of a fast-moving, competitive, stressful and polluted environment and she forgets the magical power of natural breathing.

Although breath awareness has been central to spiritual and mystical traditions throughout the ages, our technological society has little respect for such 'primitive' interests. As we search for our spiritual selves we may find ourselves turning more and more to ancient traditions and natural methods to develop our awareness of the unseen world. And what could be more natural than breathing!

Breathtaking benefits

The quality of our breathing affects our resilience and endurance, brain alertness and serenity levels. In fact the benefits of slower and deeper breathing (which we will call 'natural breathing') are absolutely *breathtaking*! They include:

- improving fitness levels

- enhancing hair and skin condition
- increasing positivity
- enhancing the ability to make decisions
- lowering high blood pressure
- increasing self-esteem
- calming nervousness
- soothing painful emotions
- clearing the mind
- strengthening resolve
- increasing energy levels
- developing tolerance and composure

EXERCISE:

The basic breath

I wonder if you resisted the temptation to try to reduce your breaths per minute to see if the results of 'eight breaths per minute or less' were all that they are cracked up to be. If you tried, using your usual breathing habits, you probably ended up gasping for breath. The only way to slow down your breathing is to use what I call 'the basic breath'. Try this now.

1. Sit on the edge of a chair with your back straight and feet on the floor. Hold your hands around your lower abdomen, one each side of your stomach.

2. Exhale fully, with a loud sigh. Deflate your stomach down to your groin and hold it empty for a few seconds.

3. Start to inhale very slowly, with your mouth closed, and feel your lower abdomen swelling in your hands. Visualize the area from your groin to your ribcage as a beautiful coloured balloon and watch and feel it inflate slowly, filling from the bottom (imagine the air coming from between your legs). Expand your balloon fully and hold for three seconds.

4. Exhale slowly, watching the balloon deflate, until your abdomen is flat.

5. Repeat for five breaths.

These steps form the basis of slow and complete breathing – natural breathing. You will experience the benefits of this exercise after only a few minutes. Keep practising daily and very soon you will be down to eight breaths a minute. Eventually, your everyday breathing patterns will change and you will find yourself experiencing new levels of confidence and self-awareness. In the future, whenever you sense your emotions getting the better of you, just start to control your breathing and feel yourself shift out of the tension zone.

Do you ever wish that you could know what someone is thinking? If only you knew their true feelings. Just think how your personal and work relationships would improve if you only knew what was going on beneath the surface. As you become increasingly aware of your own breathing patterns and start to develop deep, natural breathing, you will become fascinated with the inhalations and exhalations of the people around you. As soon as you start to focus on breathing it stops being the invisible and private process that it used to seem. If a person is nervous or angry their breaths will be weak and shallow, coming from the upper chest. Depression is characterized by heavy and laboured breathing. Fear can produce very little breathing or even holding of the breath, and happy people breathe deeply and completely. Watch and listen to your own breathing and that of others and gain amazing insights and added awareness.

A yogic breathing practice

Don't try this exercise until you have become familiar with the basic breath. It involves a rhythmic shallow breathing through the nose. Throughout the exercise focus on the inside tip of the nose, at the point where the air hits the nasal passage as you exhale.

1. Start breathing slowly, making the in-breath and the out-breath of an equal length and intensity. Don't pause between the in- and out-breaths.

2. When the inhalation and exhalation are of equal length and intensity you can begin to breathe more deeply and quickly.

3. Do this exercise for about 30 seconds and then stop and rest for a moment before you repeat it. You are advised to stick to a maximum of four 30-second rounds at each sitting.

Eventually the breath will become short and sharp with a definite feeling of impact at the points between the in-/out-/in-breaths. After two to four weeks you will notice that at the end of the exercise you will start to smell a new and pleasantly sweet smell at the tip of your nose.

Breathing exercises will change your consciousness, allowing a new spiritual awareness to pervade your life. Enjoy!

Reflections

- Our breathing changes the chemistry of our consciousness.

- When you can breathe at eight breaths a minute or less, you will become more self-assured, calmer, highly focused and healthier.

- Focus on your own breathing habits and learn to control your emotions by controlling your breath.

- Watch the breathing patterns of others and learn their state of mind.

- Breathing techniques have always been central to ancient spiritual and mystical traditions.

- Start to breathe fully and completely and you will start to live fully and completely.

37

You Can Survive

'Cooperation is as much a part of the system as competition, and the slogan "survival of the fittest" distorts this fact.'

GEORGE SOROS

Whether you love them or hate them, reality TV gameshows look as if they are here to stay. It seems that many of us find it fascinating to watch a motley crew of contestants thrash out their differences in some remote exotic environment, or even in a house in the city. It's hard enough living with your best friend or your partner and these you have *chosen* for their compatibility with you. Put a group of strangers in an enclosed situation and you have a recipe for an infinite number of unexpected dramas, and this is why many of us have switched on. These shows are pretty addictive viewing because we love to see what happens when people are forced to live and work together: tempers flare, personalities clash, attractions are inevitable – it's just like real life! Live soaps make good TV because we have an innate curiosity about others, and we can pass all our armchair judgements without having to be personally involved.

Life throws us all together in a great melting pot and we can find ourselves in many potentially difficult social situations: working with people we don't like, having to spend time with relatives who rub us up the wrong way, facing stressful situations and losing our cool, feeling criticized and misunderstood. No, we don't have to be on reality TV to need some survival tactics!

Living in harmony

Although we complain about other people, we know, deep down, that we feel at our most positive and optimistic about life when we are communicating and working successfully with others: there is nothing quite like the satisfaction that comes from achieving a team goal. Human beings are here to learn to live and to work together, and whenever we achieve this in some way, we feel really great (we reach a team target at work, for example, or our relations come together to celebrate a family event). So how can we overcome potential social discord and negotiate tricky group encounters? How can we learn to tolerate each other's differences?

Eight ways to survive

1. Always try to bring out the best in people. Remember that others are as shy as you are, and they don't always feel confident enough to show their best side. Be encouraging and supportive and you will be amazed by the effect this has.

2. But don't be a victim! Always expect others to treat you well. If you carry a sense of unworthiness about with you it is likely to draw potential bullies and victimizers into your arena.

3. Respect yourself and your ideas, and others will mirror your feelings. When you are high in self-esteem you will attract admiration and support (victimizers won't enter your orbit).

4. Check your personal boundaries. Decide how far you are prepared to go with another person and don't overstep these limits. Be clear about how far others can go with you (emotionally, spiritually, mentally and physically). This is easier than it sounds; you demonstrate your boundaries instinctively with your body language, words and attitude.

5. Be tolerant of the shortcomings of others. Not the easiest thing to do, especially as we are often irritated and annoyed by those personality and character traits of others that we ourselves share (this is often hard for us to recognize).

6. Use good communication skills. And this doesn't just mean improving your chat-up lines and persuasive arguments. When people are described as good communicators they usually have one special skill that endears them to others: they are good listeners. Listening is a dying art, and one that we need to revive if we are to make good relationships with others. Listen well and new doors will open for you. Try this today!

7. Say what you mean. Be straightforward – people appreciate it if they know where they stand with you. Don't beat about the bush. It wastes a lot of time and shows disrespect for the intelligence of others.

8. Always remember that people come first. The details of business deals, work commitments and social situations may seem vital at the time, but these scenarios come and go. The most important element of any encounter is always the personal one: people matter most. Strive for harmony and overcome discord because cooperation is at the root of all fruitful human endeavours.

Surviving a roomful of strangers

Cast your mind back to the last time you were faced with a group of strangers, perhaps at a party, a work training event or a job interview. Faced with the unknown, our adrenaline starts rushing and our behaviour can become erratic. The person who can survive the pressure is the one who has high self-esteem and feels free to be herself or himself. You know only too well what it's like to turn up to such a group event feeling nervous and low in confidence: all the others seem so much more together don't they? The truth is that everyone feels intimidated sometimes, but the person who survives and is able to overcome such feelings is the one who has an open mind and can see the lighter side of life. The pessimist will look for problems and find them, while the optimist will act spontaneously and creatively. We all know which of these two types we would want on our team.

Have you got what it takes to survive?

The following is a list of personality traits that indicate how well we cope when the pressure is on:

- Fear of rejection (negative)
- Good sense of humour, can laugh at self (positive)
- Worried about not being liked (negative)
- Genuinely likes people and shows interest in them (positive)
- Has to have the last word, must be right (negative)
- Can say sorry when necessary (positive)
- Self-centred (negative)
- Good listener (positive)
- Low self-esteem (negative)
- Doesn't take things personally (positive)

The negative characteristics will cause problems and the positive ones will clear the way and help to resolve any conflict. What are your positive traits? In what ways are you good at communicating with others and putting them at ease? Do you always say what you think or are you careful not to hurt people's feelings? Do you ever take this too far and end up never asking for anything because you are too afraid of what people will think? Are you plagued with low self-confidence and inhibitions or do you have a more laid-back approach? Can you ignore personal criticisms or are you very affected by the opinions of others?

The easiest way to eliminate the negative is simply to accentuate the positive. Work on developing the positive aspects of your character and you will find it increasingly easy to let go of any limiting negative traits.

EXERCISE:

Inner listening

We are social creatures and our lives are rooted in the expectations, needs and aspirations of the others around us. While we always need to be sensitive to the wishes of others, we must also be aware of our own needs. An optimistic, positive and upbeat approach always stems from a strong inner sense of self.

Take regular time out to tune in to your inner awareness (grab a moment in the office, on the tube, in a taxi, in the shower ... wherever). Tap into your feelings throughout the day and reflect on what is happening (*How do I feel about this? How does this decision affect me? What are my needs? Is this person good for me? ... etc.*) Make inner listening a 'must do' activity and you will find that your mind is less cluttered and that you have greater clarity in decision-making. As you develop this technique you will start to create a calm inner space where you can think things through with a welcome sense of emotional detachment. Inner listening provides a platform where you can evaluate and test your feelings and ideas, and this prevents you from over-reacting to the daily dramas of life.

Give yourself time and space to get to know your real needs. Develop your reflective skills and others will find you more approachable and friendly. Take the pressure off yourself and feel your levels of stress dropping away. You can do more than survive this life; you can enjoy it!

Reflections

- We feel at our most positive and optimistic about life when we are communicating and working successfully with others.

- When you are high in self-esteem you will attract admiration and support, and victimizers won't enter your orbit.

- We are often irritated and annoyed by those character traits of others that we ourselves share.

- Listen well and new doors will open for you.

- The most important element of any encounter is always the personal one: people matter most.

- Don't just survive, enjoy!

38

Letting Go

'When you got nothing, you got nothing to lose. You're invisible now, you got no secrets to conceal.'

BOB DYLAN

The rate of our spiritual development is directly related to our ability to let go. Letting go means releasing the worldly attachments that are holding us back. Perhaps we have outgrown certain habitual thought and behaviour patterns or we may need to release emotions that are preventing us from moving forward. As we grow spiritually, we become more and more self-aware, and it is not long before we begin to question why we do the things we do. Does playing the role of victim serve any purpose apart from allowing everyone to wipe their feet on you? Does it do you any good to feel so angry with that person who you just *cannot* and *will not* forgive? Do you really need to go around 'saving' everyone? Why do you need to be needed in this way? Does that relationship/job/attitude/lifestyle habit actually work for you any more? Are you stuck in a rut that is holding you back? What exactly are you hanging on to?

Sanaya Roman puts it this way: 'When a person, situation, or thing has taught you all it can, your Higher Self will replace it with something that will offer you new opportunities to grow and evolve.' This is a very positive and constructive way to view the changes that enter our lives. If something has passed its sell-by date, it's time to throw it out and replace it with something fresh. Letting go of the old has to happen before you can open to the new.

Getting stuck in the past

As your spiritual awareness enlightens your life, you will begin to see the places where you allow your past experiences to hold you back. Why allow past mistakes to limit you now? Haven't you punished yourself enough? So what if you have been hurt in a relationship, this doesn't mean that you can never risk being intimate again. And if you are so angry with someone that every time you think of them the adrenaline starts pumping, ask yourself this: who exactly is being punished here?

Consider this list:

- Because he let me down I can never trust another man.
- Because I was bullied at school I can't make friends now.
- Because I failed that exam I can't learn anything new.
- Because my parents criticized me I can never feel confident.
- Because I don't believe in God I cannot develop my spirituality.
- Because I did something that was wrong I deserve to be punished forever.
- Because I think that I am stupid I can't train for a new job.

And so it can go, on and on and on ... The truth is that holding on to the past (however terrible it was) serves no purpose except to carry on hurting us.

Letting go of people

This is quite a challenge. What is the difference between loving and caring and being attached? Some of you will be concerned that non-attachment must mean lack of care and compassion, but actually the reverse is true.

Think of that expression *tough love*. Parents are often called upon to be cruel in order to be kind, and to do this requires them to detach at a personality level in order to serve their child's highest need. Letting go of someone means detaching from the need to be liked and knowing that you are acting from the best and highest motives. When we are not attached we are serving people's Higher Selves rather than their personalities.

A friend of mine who has a big heart collected a vast assortment of people with problems. She used to lend money, listen all night to problems and keep an open house. When she decided to go back to college she didn't have the time, energy and money to support her network of casualties and so she had to turn needy people away. This decision was very hard for her to make because her personality identified with her role as a 'caring' person. It was a big surprise to her to discover that all of these people who had seemed so utterly dependent on her managed to find other ways to help themselves: everyone survived without her.

We cannot solve people's problems for them, and if you are trying to do that for anyone in your life at the moment, then you are attached; and if you are attached you are working at a personality level. What exactly do you get out of this relationship where someone is so dependent on you?

If you need to save people from the error of their ways you will slow up your spiritual growth. Non-attachment brings clarity and perspective to any situation. Everyone has a Higher Self, so give them the chance to resolve their own conflicts at the highest possible level. Love and let go.

Sometimes letting go means leaving. A client made this revealing disclosure about her relationship with a man who victimized her: 'I kept going back to him over and over again for six years. And then one day I just knew that he would never stop drinking and never stop treating me badly. It suddenly seemed so clear, just as if I'd taken off a blindfold. Anyway, that was it and I just got out of there and have never seen him since and that was 10 years ago.'

We can spend years of our lives locked into someone else's bad behaviour, addictions, craziness, and then, one day, we see the relationship for what it is. If we take the right action on that day our inner resources will give us all the mental, emotional and spiritual strength we need.

Before we can let go of anything (behaviour, thought, emotion, person, relationship, job) that is holding us back, we must of course recognize and accept that we are hanging on to something we have outgrown. Sometimes these attachments can be difficult to spot and it maybe years before a particular blindfold is lifted. When you are wholeheartedly in pursuit of spiritual development you are graced with added clarity and insight: your intention to expand your horizons leads you to new awareness. All you need is a strong intention to progress and the power to act appropriately when the time comes.

EXERCISE:

What are you hanging on to?

Imagine that you are holding a gigantic magnifying glass over your life. What can you see that you couldn't see before? What or whom have you outgrown? Think about the following categories:
• negative thoughts

- victim behaviour (being a doormat)

- rescuing behaviour (being a saviour)

- pessimism

- unequal relationships (being bullied or being a bully)

- low self-belief

- anger (festering)

- denial (head in the sand)

- sadness

Look through this list and see if it gives you any inspiration. Think of this as detective work: you are looking for the clues that may lead you to a solution. As soon as you recognize something that you are hanging on to, name it. Write:

I . . . . . (your name) am hanging on to . . . .

Now that it is named you are more than halfway there: recognition is awareness.

EXERCISE:

Ways to let go

Physical release

If you are hanging on to emotions there really is nothing as good as beating the hell out of a pillow. Choose a private time when the house is empty and get those feathers flying (shout, yell and really make a scene). You will be amazed at how effective this technique is. Physical release often leads on to mental and emotional clarity. Give it a go and just feel the power of that pent up energy.

Releasing the past

Make your own 'because' list, like the one on page 217. Now apply logic to this list. Why should something that happened in the past stop you from living your life to the full right now?

Pretend that this is someone else's list. What would you say to them? Choose to move on. Discard the personal garbage in your life and step forwards.

Releasing people

Yes, you can do this! Change your behaviour and the people around you will change or leave your life in some way. We teach people how to treat us, so if you are being treated badly, look to your own behaviour. If there is no option but to leave, then do it. Your spiritual development corresponds with the level at which you are being true to yourself. *Be true to yourself.*

As you take action to release a person, do the following:

- Repeat the affirmation, 'It is easy to let go.'

- Visualize the person concerned shrinking in size until they totally disappear from view.

- Every time you think of this person, let the thought go as soon as you become aware of it (people can live in our thoughts). This will become easier and easier the more you do it.

You *can* let go of people; it is entirely possible as long as you remain determined. When you let go of others they will also experience new clarity and awareness.

Reflections

- You have to let go of the old before you can open to the new.
- Holding on to the past will only keep you hurting.
- We teach people how to treat us.
- The need to 'save' people will slow up your spiritual growth.
- Love and let go.
- Be true to yourself.

39
Be Yourself

'You must see through your own mask
if you want to take it off.'

DEEPAK CHOPRA

A newborn baby comes into our world with innocence, awareness, clarity and a sure sense of self (just look into a baby's eyes
and you will see the truth of this). You were born with this
clarity; you came knowing exactly who you were. But growing
up means getting to grips with the material world and the
expectations and rules of society. As we learn to 'fit in' we
began to lose that strong connection with self. The young
child's preoccupation with gaining attention and approval leads
to 'outer directed' behaviour, which is largely dictated by the
opinions of the authority figures in its life (parents, siblings,
teachers, etc.). And so our social conditioning leads us slowly
away from our instinctive, intuitive clarity and that original
strong sense of self.

Our challenge is to become 'inner directed': to understand
and know our self; to be free of the need for approval and so to
be able to realize our full potential as a human being. The paths
to self-awareness are to be found in all aspects of our lives: at
work, in relationships, in our leisure pursuits, at home and in
whatever we do. Wherever you go you take yourself, and you

are ever-changing and developing. You are a work in progress and this piece of work will never be finished until you leave the planet. It's good to remember this at all times, and it's especially helpful when we are in a personal crisis of some sort. When we are facing our trials and tribulations it's easy to forget the bigger picture. As we focus our energy on the detail of our lives we can lose a sense of our true purpose and intention.

Behind the masks we wear

Your journey of self-discovery reveals that you are so much more than you think you are. Your self-image comprises a collection of ever-changing roles and personalities. You adopt this or that persona to deal with different situations. This doesn't mean that you are being false in some way; it is only an indication of your incredible ability to be creative and adaptable in any situation. Watch any two-year-old role-playing and you will see a potential Oscar winner. Yes, the world truly is a stage and we are creatures of infinite parts.

Two important points emerge:

- You are a naturally creative being.
- The roles you play are transient.

Once your behaviour becomes 'inner-directed' and you are focusing on your own development, the whole of your life begins to change. Someone once said that all personal growth is hard-earned and in a sense this is true. This is not to say that life is a struggle, but it does mean that each step towards a new awareness requires us to let go of an old conviction that no longer holds true. Our 'truth' at any one time is a moveable feast. What is right and true for us at one point in our lives may not be so further on down the line.

Looking back

Think back to a time in the past when you behaved in a way that you never would now. Perhaps you allowed someone to treat you badly in a relationship or maybe you didn't stand up for yourself at work. You will have plenty of your own examples – we only have to look back a few months before we are saying, 'I can't believe I did that', or 'How did I put up with that behaviour?'

1. Describe what happened and how you reacted.

2. How would you react to that situation now?

3. Why would you act differently now?

4. What was 'true' for you then that isn't 'true' for you now?

When you look back into your history you will see how far you have come and how much you have changed. As you gain new insights you start to let go of restrictive beliefs and habits, and sometimes this may mean letting go of what was once an important element of your self-image. For example, you might once have cherished the notion that you were a selfless friend who was always ready to listen to and to help others in distress. And then maybe a time comes when you feel (justifiably) irritated and used by someone who always calls you up to complain about her relationships. You may start to wonder why she never asks how you are and why she doesn't just up and leave the ghastly man she is always moaning to you about. What has happened here? Have you suddenly stopped being a good friend or have you awakened to the fact that you have changed and no longer feel the need to be victimized by the constant complaints of this person? As you begin to see through your masks, they become redundant and more and more of your true self is revealed.

Your true self

Daily life asks much of us at a physical level, and as we rush about in our quest to clock up outcomes and successes (or even just get the chores done) it is easy to believe that what you see is what you get. But, as you know, there is more to this life than meets the eye.

The real you is so much more than the physical image you see reflected in the mirror. You are a physical, emotional and spiritual being and your life needs to reflect all your amazing qualities. Self-knowledge is the key to change and it is within your power to take charge of your own life by learning to create your own reality. Recognize the link between cause and effect in everything that you do and use new positive strategies to change your behaviour and to create favourable outcomes. Let go of all blame and walk your talk; take responsibility for your part in creating the quality of your life.

Your true self is more than the sum of your parts; it is divinely linked to the universal energy source. Never ever forget your divine connection. You are never alone, even though it sometimes feels as if you are. This feeling of separation is an illusion; everything is connected. When ordinary life is getting you down and it's hard to believe that you are a fascinating creature with infinite potential and magnificent creative gifts, just reach inside yourself to your Higher Self and ask for guidance and support. As you undergo the journey of your lifetime help is at hand every single step of the way; you only ever need to ask for it!

It's always helpful to remind ourselves that every single human being is travelling their own path to awareness, even if they are not yet conscious of this. Such a reminder helps us to remain compassionate and tolerant towards others, even if their way is not our way. And when the going gets rough, try to be kind and loving towards yourself. It's so much easier to deal with personal dissatisfaction when we recognize it as a sign of divine discontent; it only means that your Higher Self is gently nudging you into some sort of transformation (you have outgrown your old self).

Love the fascinating journey to find the true self that lies behind the paraphernalia of your life. Take away the props and stage apparel, remove the masks and what do you find? You discover a beautiful soul who is striving to live her best life at all times.

References and Further Reading

Cameron, Julia, *The Vein of Gold*, Pan Books, 1997

Carlson, Richard, *Don't Sweat the Small Stuff*, Hodder and Stoughton, 1998

Dass, Ram, *Remember Be Here Now*, Hanuman Foundation, 1980

De Angelis, Barbara, *Are You the One for Me?*, Thorsons, 1998

Dickinson, Emily, *Everyman's Poetry*, Orion, 1999

Field, Lynda, *Creating Self-Esteem*, Vermilion, 2001

    The Self-Esteem Workbook, Vermilion, 2001

    Self-Esteem for Women, Vermilion, 2001

    Just Do it Now, Vermilion, 2001

Gawain, Shakti, *Living in the Light*, Eden Grove Editions, 1988

Gibran, Kahlil, *The Prophet*, Heinemann, 1970

Hay, Louise, *You Can Heal Your Life*, Eden Grove Editions, 1988

Heidelck, Susanne, *Insight Pocket Book Guide to Rhodes*, APA Publications, 1999

Huffines, LaUna, *Bridge of Light,* H.J. Kramer Inc., 1993

Lang, Doe, *The Charisma Book*, Wyden Books, 1980

Peale, Norman Vincent, *You Can If You Think You Can*, Cedar Books, 1974

Roman, Sanaya, *Personal Power Through Awareness*, H. J. Kramer, Inc., 1986

    Spiritual Growth, H.J. Kramer, Inc., 1989

Ruiz, Don Miguel, *The Four Agreements*, Amber-Allen
    Publishing, Inc., 1997

Schaef, Anne Wilson, *Meditations for Women Who do too
    Much*, HarperCollins, 1996

Schultz, Mona Lisa, *Awakening Intuition*, Bantam Books, 1999

Vanzant, Iyanla, *Until Today*, Pocket Books, 2001

Thank you also to the Hanuman Foundation for permission
to reproduce text from *Remember Be Here Now*, copyright ©
Hanuman Foundation, 1980.

Index